Elder Story 4
What We Did

Compiled and Edited by

Gordon A. Long

AIRBORN PRESS
Delta, B. C.

ElderStory 4
What We Did

Published by
AIRBORN PRESS
4958 10A Ave, Delta, B. C.
V4M 1X8
Canada

Copyright Gordon A. Long
2018

All rights reserved, including the right to reproduce this book or any portion thereof in any form without the express written permission of the publishers. These stories remain the intellectual property of the storytellers.

ISBN: 978-1-988898-06-3
Printed by CreateSpace

Cover Design by Tania Mendoza
Cover Photo by Cathy Yeulet

Other Books in This Series:

ElderStory 1: Who We Were
ElderStory 2: Who We Are
ElderStory 3 Where We Came From
Available at most online retailers

For the Families

This is a book of real stories about real people. ElderStory has requested that, wherever possible, storytellers get permission from people to use their names and stories. The stories remain the intellectual property of the storytellers. It is our hope and desire that no one will be hurt or offended by his or her portrayal in any of these tales.

For the Storytellers

These stories as published may not be exactly the same as the story you usually tell. It is the nature of folk tales that they change over time. You tell the story differently each time. People remember it differently. In the process of recording/transcribing/editing, things get changed, especially if there is translation involved. But the story is still your story, and it is a story that people want to hear.

Thanks To

John Lusted and the KinVillage Association in Tsawwassen

Morgan Gadd, for his expertise and support.

Staff, students and families of Ecole Woodward Hill Elementary School, especially Lisa Anderson, Ravinder Grewal, Jas Kooner, Kelly Mcquillan and of course Elaine Vaughan, who organized our sessions.

Staff, students and families of Surrey Central Elementary School, especially principal James Pearce, and Sean Austin, John Kovach, Kevin Larking and Grace Jackson.

Staff and residents at the Langley Lodge Care Home

Pamela Chestnut, Mona, Tania Mendoza and Mercedes at DIVERSEcity.

In Memorium

We would like to dedicate this book to the memory of two of our participants who have passed away since telling us their stories.

When you read about their lives in this and other ElderStory books, please take a moment to think of

Maggie Gooderham

Cal Whitehead

and the contributions they have made to Canada over their many years in this country.

Introduction

The ElderStory Project came about in a very natural way. So many people deeply regret not making a record of their family's stories before it was too late. And so those stories died with the people who told them.

Those of us on the Surrey Seniors Planning Table looked for a way to keep family stories moving down through the generations. It is good for children to know where they come from, who their families are. It leads to a sense of belonging and a stronger sense of self worth.

So we sought ways to enhance the telling of stories to keep family members and communities in contact with each other. And the ElderStory Project was born, with the intention of bringing the generations together through storytelling.

Our storytellers come from all walks of life, from all ages, from many cultural groups. Their histories originate in communities in rural Canada: in small villages in India and Iraq: in large towns and big cities around the world. But wherever they originate, the message always comes out the same. "Now we are here, and much though we love the places we came from, in this place we are happy."

The Surrey Seniors' Planning Table and DIVERSEcity Community Resources Society hope that you will enjoy these very Canadian stories.

Contents

Daily Life All Over – 1

Other Places, Other Times – 23

In the Military – 41

A Full Life – 54

Family Lore – 65

The Perfect Storm – 76

Book 4 Participants – 97

Daily Life All Over

1. ## Joan Campbell – Coming to Canada

   I was a war bride, so that dates me. I came on the Queen Mary on her last trip before she was turned back into a luxury liner. There were 1500 of us with our babies and children. We arrived in Halifax. We were looked after beautifully by the Red Cross. It was a wonderful trip.

   When we arrived there was a band playing and a lot of people there. It was very exciting, and we were all lined up on the side. This new country we were coming to, you know.

   And then the Minister of Agriculture stood up, and he said, "We are very proud to welcome such fine breeding stock." We stood and looked at each other, and here we were with one, two, three, or four children each.

   Anyway, that made us laugh. It was just so exciting. I found that the sound of the trains was different from any trains in England, and everything was so exciting. I never regretted it for one moment ever, coming to Canada. Such a wonderful country. So I'm pleased to be here.

2. ## Eva – Life in Mexico

   My name is Eva. My father is Andres. My mother is Perdrita. When I was eight years old my mother died. My sister was 14 years old and I was eight. We were only with our father. My father remarried two years after my mother died, and my sister got married, too.

   We had a store. We worked hard because my father never went to school. My sister started a business and she got married. When my father got married again, I needed to help him, too. I had been at school for two years, and my teacher taught me Mathematics, and she taught me a great deal. My teacher wanted me to get to Grade 5 because I was very good at Mathematics.

   I only studied until Grade 4. Then my father got married and I couldn't continue to study. I needed to help him in the business. I worked hard. After 7 years of marriage his wife died again, leaving me with two children. Then I needed to survive with my father and two more brothers. But the same person who gave us merchandise for the business supported me to increase the business. This is the way I learned how to support my father and my brothers. When I got married, my brothers were 17 and 18 years old. Then they started looking for work, and after they became 22 years old they got married.

Then I supported my brothers like a mother, to get married, and my husband helped them. I give thanks to God that I have a very good husband. We are 61 years married. Never has he told me anything bad, always treating me with care and love. And he helped me to continue because my husband doesn't want me to get sick.

I have two daughters, one son. God gave us the opportunity, and these children got married. My two daughters came to Canada to study English.

I was crying because they were in Canada. Afterwards they told me they were going to get married in Canada. My son got married in Mexico, and they told him to come to Canada. Then I came to Canada with my son, because we were alone in Mexico. When the three of them got married, now, after so many years, we have been in Canada for 8 years. We have our citizenship already.

I have been in Canada, and I feel the spirit was from my husband. I give thanks to God for this blessing. This is a very good life with my husband. Everything that happened a long time ago when I found my husband I felt peace and happiness. This is why I love him so much.

3. Eve Baldwin – Introduction

I was born in 1925. That makes me 92. Can you believe it? When I was about 4 months old I went to India with my father and I had an amah out there. I had the same amah all the time I was there. She was more like a mother to me. I had an adopted mother in England. It's very complicated. I'm trying to find out my parentage now, and I have people delving as far as they can but everything is classified, and I can't find anything out.

My adopted father never knew anything about me, and my adopted mother, who was originally my nanny (but I called her my mother) in England, she did know but she died without telling me. I found out who my mother was, but my father, I cannot find, and I have people desperately trying to find out, but they have come up blank.

I went with my adopted father because I adored him. But often he would bring me back to England He wanted me to keep a lot of

English in me because I was going wild in India. I became almost a feral child out there. He wanted me there, so I was left on my own a lot.

Then I would go to England and stay with the adopted grandmother and go to school in England for a while, and I would go backwards and forwards.

Then my father decided I would go to boarding school. So at 11 years old I went to the Red Maid boarding school in Bristol.

It was a horrendous change for me to be amongst a lot of girls in the boarding school, but we had a wonderful end room with an outside fire escape. And we got to know the boys in the next-door boys' school very well, and that's how I met my husband. He said he saw me climbing a tree and all he could see was black bloomers up there.

He said, "I'm going to marry you one day."

I said, "Okay," and that was it. We did get married. But that's another story.

There were four of us in this little room. We used to have midnight snacks and everything. I got to know them very well, and they got to know me very well, because I could always tell them a story.

We got on very well. We were fast friends right to the end. They've all died now.

This was a wonderful boarding school. I loved it there. One of my friends became a day girl because her father had died, and I lived at her house as a day girl, but I wanted to go back to boarding because I enjoyed it more. I don't know why, but I really enjoyed boarding school. I didn't think I would, but I did.

I enjoyed the camaraderie and company of the girls, which I had never really had.

4. Eve Baldwin – Coming to Canada

I met my real best friend, Red, in 1944 in Singapore. I was going on holiday for a week, and we didn't know each other. She was on the train and I was running for the train, because it had just started.

I had my small kit bag, and she said, "Throw it!"

So I threw it. She caught it and grabbed my hand and pulled me in. That handclasp was our friendship until the day she died. She died about six years ago, which was heartbreaking for me.

When I got back to England the biggest surprise of my life, I got married and everything else, and I was corresponding with Red, and then she was coming to England, and she was going to Bristol, so I met her at a designated place. I said, "Come over tomorrow to my husband's house for supper."

So she came over the next night with her new husband and rang the bell, and my husband went to the door and said, "Red!"

I said, "You know each other?"

She said, "Yes, we were together in Singapore."

I said, "I didn't even know that!"

So the four of us together decided we'd emigrate to Canada. So in 1956 they went to Canada, but we went to Nigeria.

The job in Nigeria was good. "Okay we can live on the allowance they gave us there, and the English money goes in the bank."

Then we came home from Nigeria, and we said, "Canada." But then the Trinidad job came up.

We said, "Okay, the same thing. Keep that money."

So we were okay when our money finally came out here.

When we came to Canada, I'd never had a job, I'd never worked, but we could only bring 3,000 pounds with us, because the rest was locked in the bank in England.

We rented a place, and I had to find a job. "Oh, dear. What can I do?"

I went to the people with the temporary business office. I said, "Can you give me a temporary job?" So they sent me to Bapco Paint. I went to Bapco in August as a temporary, and they said to me, "On January 1 we're starting our own payroll. Would you like to do the payroll?"

I turned to the girl sitting next to me and said, "What's payroll?"

She said, "I'll tell you later."

So I said, "Okay, I'll do that."

So I went down to Terminal Avenue for a day's training, and I stayed at Bapco ICI until they folded up and went back to Toronto. There were too many managers and nobody to do the work.

It was fun while I worked there. I still keep in touch with friends I worked with. But that's the only job I ever had. Then as soon as we got our money from England and we paid off our mortgage, we were all right.

Lots of people couldn't get their money out. I don't know why England did that. It was like our pension, you know? I know the cost of living increased a lot in England.

5. Roger Barnes – Love at First Sight

My name is Roger Barnes. I was born in Widnes, England in 1946. Close to the Liverpool/Manchester area. My Father was a tradesman, but he had an accident to his hands, so he couldn't work at his trade anymore, so then he worked in an office.

My story started off in early June, 1971. I was on my vacation from my job. I used to work for Imperial Chemical Industries Saltworks, in Runcorn, England. I was running the weigh scale for the trucks that came into the plant. Later I worked in the payroll office.

I was supposed to pick up a friend at the local train station in Runcorn. The person I was supposed to pick up was the grandchild of friends of my parents. Her name was Thalia Margaret Nowazek. Her grandparents had lived two doors down from my parents in Runcorn, Cheshire, England, but they moved to British Columbia. She was coming on a holiday from British Columbia, travelling with her grandparents.

I picked them up and took them to my parents' home, which was two doors down from her grandparents old house. The next day I asked Thalia to come to Liverpool, and to see a lighthouse that was close to Liverpool, and she said that was okay.

While we were in Liverpool, you may think it's really strange, but I asked her to marry me. You never see these stories anymore. She said that was okay.

In August, when her vacation was over, we agreed that we would meet again, say in October. So around November of that year Thalia came over from British Columbia. We talked about getting married. The day we talked about was in November.

We tried to get Thalia's Mum and Dad over to England, but that wasn't possible. They couldn't come for the wedding. But it was a great wedding day. We were both very happy on this great day. We picked Blackpool in Lancashire for our honeymoon, even though it rained all the time we were there. But that was okay. We were both very happy.

It was just unbelievable that everything happened so quickly. But you never hear about these things happening for real.

We had two sons, one who lives in Edmonton and the other in Aldergrove.

6. Jamie Long – Amigo

By the time I was about 13 or so, Maude and Star, the logging horses, had been pensioned off to live a happy life, I think they went up to Dad's homestead, and they were basically turned loose to have a lazy retirement with no encumbrances at all.

I was at an age when I needed a horse. So Dad hears about this Range Band horse way out in the far reaches of Wisteria, which was way out past Francois Lake. It was supposed to be a palomino – white mane and copper-coloured body – three years old and never been ridden.

Somehow or other my Dad finds out about this horse, and he finds out the guy who owns the horse had hardly even seen it, and there was a small transaction of money done, and we were allowed to go and hook up with this horse that was running with a band of wild horses.

We took my Uncle Ray with us. Uncle Ray was a rodeo rider and a fine horseman himself. He had a pickup with a horsebox on it, so we went out, way out the far end of Francois :ake and into Wisteria, and into the timber to try to hunt down this Range Band set of horses. And sure enough we did find them. It took us three days, and we had a real rodeo trying to get them rounded up and whatever else. We had started on Thursday, and on Sunday we finally got a rope on the horse we ended up calling Amigo. We got a rope on Amigo, and Ray proceeded to try to get him into the pickup.

Well, that was a no-go. That horse was wild as wild could be. He was 16 hands high. He was a big strong horse, a quarter horse, but Ray said, "Well, we'll fix this."

So he got a Come-along and he tied it to the bullboard of his pickup and we winched the horse, skidding, into the back of the truck. And that horse kicked the livin' daylights out of that pickup. I didn't know what was gonna break first, that horse's feet or the back of the pickup.

But anyway, we got Amigo home. And was he ever fine. Not only was he beautiful, but once we started to know him, he was just a dear. He was so much fun. He was always looking for sugar, because I always had sugar cubes in my pocket to spoil him, and Dad did, too. But he'd stick his big velvety nose in your ear, and he'd blow in your ear, and then he'd pull your hat off and go running away with it, and all sorts of fun.

We were slow breaking him. My Dad said, "We're not hard breaking him. We'll just get him used to the saddle, and used to the bridle, and finally get him to the point where we can ride him.

So we did this for about six months, right through the winter, and I had really grown to love that horse like you'd never believe, and my Dad loved him, too. He was really a fine horse, and he was proving up to be great.

I could get up on him, but I couldn't ride him. I could get the saddle on, then put my body across the saddle without actually getting in, and he'd tolerate that, but then he'd start to buck me off. He'd take the bridle pretty well, and so that worked out pretty good.

This was in the spring of the year by this time, and I think I was 13 or 14. It was a Saturday, and I was going to see if I could get up on him. I kinda had the plan to get up on him that day. So I got the bridle on him and I got the saddle on him.

Now, Amigo had about an acre that was fenced off, with the barn in it, and that's what his area was. We didn't have an actual corral that we could put him in, which we shoulda had. But anyway what happened was that he was kinda feeling his oats; it was springtime. So I get the bridle on him and I get the saddle up on him and I'm about to tie the girth up tight, and darned it all he breaks away from me and goes galloping off, and I didn't have the girth done up full shot.

Well, sure enough, guess what happens. The saddle slipped underneath him, and he went wild. He kicked and he was wrecking the saddle, and I was doing everything I could, trying to stop him.

Finally the bugger comes up to me and he stops. Great. I grabbed hold of the bridle, I had ahold of him, and with one hand I reached over and undid the cinch and got it undone, I started to pull the saddle off. Soon as I got that saddle off he broke loose from me and goes gunning around, gunning around, just running, getting lathered up like crazy.

By this time Dad had showed up, and he says, "I tell you what we'll do. We'll take the lariat and stake it out in front of the barn door and see if we can run him into the barn so we can catch him."

Well he goes gunnin' full shot, right through the flippin' rope and got all tangled up in that and went even more crazy. He did about two or three more passes around the paddock there goin' full shot, and he goes gunnin' up to the fence and he jumps the fence, down the driveway and out onto Highway 16, the Yellowhead, and Whambo! The old mail truck to Alaska nailed him and killed him dead, just like that.

I heard the screech of the truck and the smack of the horse, and I ran for the gun. I grabbed the 30-30, and I go runnin' out there, and my Dad said to me. "You won't be needin' that," he said. It was the meanest thing that a guy could ever say to a heartbroken kid. I'll tell you that for sure, that was a hardship for me. But I'll tell you what it was, my Dad was hurtin' so bad himself over losin' the horse.

So anyway that's fine, I went to bed. That was it for me. I was absolutely totally depressed.

So in the morning about 11 o'clock I guess, I clawed myself out of bed, all mopey and Mum comes up to me, "Well, Honey," she says, "You'd better say your last words to Amigo, because Dad's going to take him out with the Cat and the stoneboat and bury him."

So I go out there to the horse at the side of the road. It only did $600 damage to the mail truck but it destroyed the horse. I went out there and Dad had skinned the horse. I think it did something to me psychologically, you know?

Turns out Dad wanted to make a set of chaps out of this beautiful hide. It was so beautiful. And we did. We had a tanning tank that we could do about nine hides at a time. Dad decided to tan him black. We tanned the hide black and it was beautiful. It was golden hair and black hide, and it was gorgeous. But you know, he never did get around to making that set of chaps out of it.

After Dad had died, years later, when we were cleaning out the old shed that was filled to the roof with crap, here's all this old hide tied up, and there, all moth-eaten and rat-chewed, there was Amigo's hide. So it was kind of a total waste all round.

That was one of the hardships I had, I'll tell you. It did something to me in the end.

7. Marilyn Gerald – Introduction

My name is Marilyn Gerald. I was born in Edmonton Alberta, August 7, 1940 to Helen and Wes VanDeusen. At least, that's what I was told. I had two sisters, Aleta and Tanis, and a step-brother, Len Hardy. My father and mother were the founders of Acme Novelty Company in Edmonton.

I went to school at Garneau Elementary School in Edmonton, and my dear, dear friend Gracie lived across the street. She was my friend from the time we were three years old.

I've been married twice. The first time to George Gerald of Edmonton. His family owned the Shasta Café, which was a 24-hour restaurant. Mr. Gerald was a Greek, and very kindly would treat all the firefighters. If there was a fire, he would treat them to meals in his restaurant.

My second marriage was in Hawaii, to John P. Sperling, who had been a naval officer. That marriage lasted for about ten minutes.

I have two wonderful, wonderful children. Carly is now 48 and has four children. Adam is 44 and he has two little boys. Tomorrow I am going to Joseph's seventh birthday party.

While I was living in Hawaii and got divorced rather quickly from my husband, I started to sell real estate. But Hawaii became very dull for me. I was lying on the beach one day looking up at the palm trees, and they almost looked plastic. I thought, "What am I doing here? What am I doing here?"

My children were going to a private school. My daughter was in Grade 5 and I realized she didn't know how to tell time. So I went and asked the teacher how come she does not know how to tell time.

"Oh, the clock broke."

I said, "When did the clock break?"

She said, "About three years ago."

I said, "Okay." She could read digital, but she couldn't read a proper clock. Report cards generally read, "Carly has a beautiful smile and does a beautiful hula." And that was sort of what she was graded on. In Science they built volcano things and blew them up. The education was not quite what I thought it should be.

My father sold Acme Novelty to Jim Pattison. He always wanted to travel, so he bought a travel agency.

He phoned me. He was having staff problems at his travel agency. He said, "Is there any way you would come back and help with the agency?"

So I did. I came back at the age of 44. My children weren't small anymore. Carly was in Grade 8 and Adam was in Grade 4.

So we came back to Canada and I went to work in the travel agency for minimal wages. I mean, it was dreadful what he was paying me.

One day my sister said, "Are you in charge of staff?"

I said, "Well…yes."

"So give yourself a raise."

So I said, "Yes, that sounds like a pretty good idea." So I boosted myself up about a hundred dollars a month or something real good.

I adored my father, but working for him was not a good experience. We were not a good employer-employee situation. So one day I quit. Just quit.

He didn't talk to me for about six months.

He had always told my sister, who still lived in Edmonton, how smart I was and what a great job I did. But he never told me.

I asked him one day, "Why don't you ever tell me?"

He said, "Because you know."

So I was walking down the street in Kerrisdale. I'd lost a lot of weight, and I was looking good. And I ran into him, and he said, "Marilyn, you look beautiful." It went through my mind that I always wanted him to say "smart," but I think I'll settle for "beautiful." Beautiful's good.

So, anyway, he said, "Why don't we sit down and talk about what you're going to do."

So I decided I'd go back and work in outside sales for his travel agency, earning commission. He had boxes and boxes of old files in the back, of previous clients that were no longer clients. So I said to him, "Can I go through these boxes and phone these people and see if I can get them as clients?"

He said, "Well, sure."

I was earning a 40% commission, and one of my pay cheques for the month was $8,000.

And he went, "This is a mistake. This has to be a mistake. Nobody earns eight thousand dollars a month at 40% commission."

So he called in the accountant, this other girl that had replaced me, and she said, "No, that's what she earned. That's what business she did."

So that was a great achievement for me. I turned out to be a sales person.

8. Marilyn Gerald – My Short Marriage.

My short marriage was to John Spierling. This was a guy who was 6 foot 3 and looked like John Wayne. And acted like John Wayne, actually. The marriage was short, but we remained good friends. John, unlike my first husband, was funny, funny, funny. I have never laughed so much in my entire life.

When he first met my family, my father said, "Hello, John, pleased to meet you."

He said, "That's what you think."

John had quite a history. He was a playboy in Honolulu. I was his third wife. He had dated Jacqueline Onassis and was mentioned in her book as one of her dates. I think he is referred to as a Honolulu businessman.

The company he was associated with owned the Mark Hopkins Hotel in San Francisco. So when we travelled to the Mark Hopkins we were in a beautiful suite. They also owned the Regent of Fiji in Fiji, and we travelled there as well. It was a very, very glamorous life. John would phone me and say, "Do you have any plans for lunch?"

I'd say, "No."

He'd say, "Meet me at the helicopter pad at the Hilton hotel," and we'd go over to Maui and have lunch.

So it was all very glamorous. I had two husbands and I loved them both very much. In a different way, but I loved both of them.

John unfortunately died. The story is that he had taken Viagra and he was with a couple of hookers in a hotel in San Francisco. And I find that quite believable.

We went to his funeral, and I met a charming young man, and I asked him what his association was with John, and he said, "I'm his lawyer."

I said, "Oh, that's interesting."

He said, "What was your association?"

I said, "I was married to John."

He said, "John was never married."

I said, "Well, I was number three."

He was a new young lawyer. He wasn't the lawyer I knew when I was with John. It was as if I'd been married to a stranger when I heard the stories and I met his brother at the funeral. They were talking about John being a graduate from Pennsylvania University, and his brother turned to me and said, "That's bullshit. He never graduated from any university."

It was all quite funny. But I had a lot of fun, a lot of laughs, and I met a lot of interesting people through John. His company was instrumental in building the Kahala Hilton, so every Saturday and Sunday our days were spent at the Kahala Hilton on the beach. We met lots of stars and it was very glamorous. It was an interesting life.

My children travelled with us a couple of times to San Francisco and once to Fiji.

Unfortunately we had some incompatibilities. I don't think you want to know about it. So I decided to divorce. He told me, "You can't afford to divorce me."

It was a very expensive divorce for me. I had to pay him to get out of the marriage. It was a lesson to be learned. But I don't hold grudges. He was what he was, and it was take it or leave it. And I left.

9. Mavis Holt – Introduction

My full name is Mavis Bertha Caroline Holt. I was named after my two grandmas. I was born in Wainwright Alberta, between Alberta and Saskatchewan on the border. I'm 80 years old. Born in 1937.

I was raised in Kamloops. I came there as a teenager. We all moved to Kamloops. My Dad worked on the CNR.

Then we moved from Kamloops to Vancouver in the fifties. Then we moved to Surrey. Then when my Dad passed away Mum and I moved to Langley.

No kids. I'm single. I never took any training or further education.

I just stayed home with my Mum. She needed looking after.

My Mum and I had an apartment. When my Mum passed away my sister-in-law put me in here (Langley Lodge) because she didn't want me to be by myself. It's a nice place, with nice people. That's why she put me in here.

When we were teenagers, my Dad and Mum took us on a holiday. We drove back to Alberta and stayed with my relations. My Mum and I went on a bus tour to California. We also went to Hawaii. Hawaii is nice. I like it. But you have to fly to Hawaii.

My Mum and I went on three tours. They pick you up, and you meet other people on the bus. We went to Disneyland. I loved Disneyland. I'd like to see Disneyland again. Then my Mum and I went to Arizona. That's the first time I saw Arizona. I have a cousin there. I don't know if he's still there or not. I haven't heard.

Nowadays I do a lot of volunteering. I look after the birds. We have a new cage, now. There used to be two cages. One bird was in one cage, and two in the other. Now we got a new cage to put all three of them in. I also put the teacups together. That's it.

10. John Palen – Intro

My name is John Palen, and I was born Dec 1, 1922, in the Village of Halliburton, Ontario, roughly 150 miles northeast of Toronto. I grew up there. My Dad worked as a railway postal clerk on the trains in the days when they did the sorting on the train. He got a job in the train running between Lindsey and Halliburton.

So he came up to Halliburton and that's where he met my mother, who was the daughter of Johnny Lucas who operated the Grand Central Hotel on the main street of Halliburton. They had three girls and three boys in their family.

Anyway, in 1932 when Dad got transferred to the Toronto Regional Postal Services, he was still a mail clerk, but operating out of Toronto. So I was going on 10 years old, and we moved to the big city of Toronto. One of the things that struck me, as a kid, even; I couldn't get over all the homes that were for sale. They had home-made signs on the lawn, "House for Sale, $2,000." "House for Sale, $1,500." Beautiful solid brick homes, 7 or 8 rooms, nice driveways, garages, nice big back yards. All for sale. Of course the Great Depression was on.

My Dad had a steady job all during the Depression, and as you know from reading history, the Great Depression started in 1929 and it went on to 1939 when the war started.

The Federal government of Canada under R. B. Bennet at the time didn't have any money to give to the provinces, and so the provinces didn't have any money to give to the municipalities. Practically every municipality in Canada was bankrupt.

But come war, they found millions of dollars in the first six months to build an army and tanks and airplanes and ships. Everything.

In 1942 I finished my schooling in Toronto. I started at Norway Public School on Kingston Road, and then I went to Danforth Tech. I graduated in a Chemistry course, and that's when I joined the Air Force.

11. David Barregar – An Interesting Life

My name is David Barregar. I was born in Rouleau, in the French part of Saskatchewan, on 29 December, 1933, to Anglophone parents. In school I played hooky. My father's name is still in the city rolls for the Saskatchewan Wheat Pool. He was instrumental in the forming of the Wheat Pool. He was a grain buyer for the Saskatchewan Wheat Pool

During my teenage years I competed in tryouts for the 1948 Olympics in swimming. Backstroke. But I didn't quite get all the way. I was in the last tryouts.

After that, in 1951 I joined the Canadian Air Force in Regina. In the beginning I did photo-interpretation and mapping Canada.

Then afterwards I met my wife in Ottawa in 1956. She was my first passenger in a little two-seater taildragger. We got married in October of 56.

By that time I was in the Intelligence Section. I was transferred to France, to Metz in the Alsace-Lorraine. We stayed four years there. Our two girls were born there. Then I was called to go to Whitehorse in Yukon Territory from 1960 to 1962, where Michael, our son, was born.

Because the Wall went up in 1962, I was called back to Germany, to Zweibrueken in the Pfalz area, still in Intelligence. There we stayed 6 years until we came back to Canada.

When we got back, I went with Rogers Oil Company selling home heating oil. From 68 to 70. for a while, and then I joined the Stock Exchange as a broker.

In 1973 I joined CBC Calgary as announcer on radio and television. The first two years I had "David Barregar's Calgary." Then there was "Four Today." I interviewed hundreds of people. That lasted until the 1988 Olympics. I also created the show, "Wild Rose Country."

I was recognized across Canada, because anything I sent out over the telex wouldn't need proofreading or checking. It was perfect.

Some of the documentaries that I was working on went worldwide. Sometimes we had people come to Vancouver and all of a sudden they would say, "Mister, say your name again. I recognize that voice." Even people from Australia and South Africa recognized my voice.

After that we had a business called "Hall of Names," that we joined when we moved to Vancouver in 1988.

12. Cal Whitehead – The Strap

Hmm...ok, when I was in grade school the students, many of them feared the strap. That was the punishment if you were caught doing something you shouldn't. You would be sent into the cloakroom. I don't think they have cloakrooms anymore, where we hung our coats. And the teacher had a large razor strap and you were to hold out your hand the teacher would strap it. And if you pulled back suddenly, you got 2 more straps.

I only got that once and it was in grade 3. I was fully bored stiff with what the teacher was saying, and I'd conceived an idea of a ruler on my desk and rubber eraser at the end of it. And if I bashed one end, the rubber would fly up and go out that window which was open about a foot. And I did this and there was a moment of silence and then the teacher came down the aisle. She passed me; I was so relieved, but then she picked me up by the ear and carried me to the cloakroom.

"Hold out your hand."

Well, I am left handed, so I held my right hand. And I got 2 strap blows. That was the only time I was punished. I was not Mr. Goody, but I adjusted to the school system. Many kids were proud of how many times they were strapped and they welcomed the punishment. I wondered later what the magic was.

It didn't hurt that much. Enough to make you not want it again. So that was the strap. Yeah.

13. Norm Schmidt – High School.

I was still living at home, and when High School time came, somehow I got registered at Kitsilano High School. I was in Kerrisdale, far, far out of their enrollment area. Unfortunately, it was an idea of keeping an eye on Norm. My dad was a teacher there.

Many items came up. 4 o'clock in the afternoon my Dad would say, "I heard that..." Somehow the Mafia in the school had let him in on what was happening.

I was not a good student. I honestly have to say that I guess about Grade 9 I had excellent marks, but on one occasion my mother had a couple of her friends in, and she said, "Norm, go and get your report card."

It suddenly occurred to me that the work I was doing at school wasn't for me; it was for my mother. However I was able to get through with a minimum amount of work, but a lot of extra-curricular activities. Especially the class newspaper, My family before my Dad ran a German-language newspaper in Ontario until such time as the new Germans coming over as immigrants they all learned to speak English, so we were redundant.

There were a million extra-curricular activities, some legitimate, some more seedy. That was when my Dad made me aware that he was watching, and there were rules to follow.

14. Cal Whitehead – More school Stories

I don't remember much more about Grade 1 than I've already told, and Grade 2. But Grade 3 was something else for me. That's when we learned how to write with pen and ink. I was left handed, and my mother had told that school, under no circumstances was I to be turned into a right-handed person. The pen nib kept digging into the cheap paper and splattering all over the place. The teacher kept pouring more ink into my inkwell, and I would go home covered with ink and scrub it off. I learned how to print more than write. That was Grade 3.

Well, I forgot all about that, and I just made my own achievement. I covered the phases of the moon and the tides in Vancouver, and the shipping, particularly two Dutch-American ships called *Oranji* and something else, and I tracked them in their journeys down to Hawaii, Fiji, New Zealand and Australia. And they'd radio back, and I'd know from the tiny little slivers in the Shipping News where they were and what they were doing.

I even got a glimpse of the *Oranji* where it was docked: 12,000 tons, with very rusty and mismatched painting. One day it was docked right beside an Empress boat. Pristine white. Everything was white. And I said, "I love my ship anyway."

Our teacher in Grade 7 was only about 18 years old, fresh out of Normal School.

One day after recess there was this funny smell in the room. And Miss Newcome said, "Who's been eating garlic?"

Elmo and his buddies stood up like heroes, you know.

Miss Newcome fell into tears, and the girls all got around her and hugged her and chewed out those boys with words that weren't in the syllabus. Oh, those boys expected to be honoured, but boy, they were chewed out very well.

15. Bernadette Law – A Tale of Two Families

I was a schoolteacher in Hong Kong, majoring in Art, and I wanted to further my studies, so I came to Canada. But when I got to Canada, I had less than $100 left after paying my airfare and my tuition fees and so on. The school knew my financial situation and they found a baby-sitting job for me so that I didn't have to worry about room and board, and I also got $5 a week. That was enough for me to buy my art supplies.

I started working after school, and when I got home from school there were 5 children, and they all came to me and hugged me and kissed me. The youngest one, 9 months old, was in a playpen. So the eldest boy would pick up the youngest brother and give him to me, and say, "This is Bernadette's boy."

After that, they would play by themselves, and I went into the kitchen and helped Mrs. Scurfield to peel potatoes and anything she wanted me to do. While I was in the kitchen, Mrs. Scurfield always asked questions about my school and my teachers and my friends. She was just like a sister and a very good friend to me, because she always wanted to know about me.

About 5 o'clock Mr. Scurfield came home, and all the kids went to the father and he picked up every kid and kissed them and put them down. I called that happy hour, because during suppertime the children talked to the father and told them what they'd done at school and at home, and it was such a happy time for them. Mrs. Scurfield seldom talked at that time, because she wanted it to be a time that the children communicated with their father.

Occasionally she would say something, like "How about the dog?"

"Oh, yes, Johnny had four puppies and they invited us to go over there and we had such a good time."

After dinner I cleaned up everything and the mother bathed the children and then the father tucked them to bed and told them a story.

It was such a warm family, happy, and there was a lot of love.

At weekend they went out and they said, "I'm so happy that you're our babysitter. The children love you and we feel comfortable, going out." Mrs. Scurfield told me, "I'm a mother, and I don't just sit and watch my children. I do my laundry and so on. You can do your studies while the children play by themselves. But you have to have your ears open. If it is too noisy you have to check what is happening, and if it is too quiet you should check as well. The rest of the time you can do your homework as long as you keep your ears open."

So the first day when they went out, I took my paper and paint and everything out and I thought I could do my homework.

When the children saw the paper and paint, they said, "Oh, what are you doing?"

They said, "Oh. We can draw. We can paint. Let us help you with your homework."

Well, that was the biggest mistake I made. They all gathered around the table, and they had a good time. I stayed with them and talked with them and we had a good time.

When they all went to bed, and the baby cried, so I held him and gave him the milk. He drank it so fast, but when there was about a quarter left he started to slow down and look at me and try to reach me with his hands, and wanted to touch me and try to talk to me, baby talk. I tried to talk to him, and it was such a good feeling. I took the time to build up a bond of love and trust. Children learn when they try to communicate with you, and this was a good thing for me.

During the weekend Mrs. Scurfield asked me to go out with friends of my age. "Don't just stay at home."

I said, "I don't have any place to go."

She said, "We're going swimming, do you want to go with us?" or "We're going curling, and we go this and that."

So I went with them.

When they went out at night on the weekend, until 12 o'clock or 1 o'clock I didn't mind, because they said, "We have confidence in you and we know the children love you, so we can go out and enjoy the evening."

Mrs. Scurfield always told me "I don't mind that the children love you so much, because I love my children, and they learn to extend their love to other people.

Which is really right.

Sometimes the children would say, "I love Bernadette, and I love China." They talked to me and I was just part of the family. I really enjoyed my time.

I worked for them until April and the college was finished, and during the summer I got a job in Waterton, at the Prince of Wales Hotel.

When I got the job at Waterton Lakes for the summertime, Mrs. Scurfield told me. "When you come back, you should go and find another job and be with people of your age and enjoy college life, and don't be stuck in a family."

I said, "Okay,"

But I looked for another babysitting job. There was another family with 5 kids. I thought that was perfect. I could handle that.

When I went there the first day outside there was a tree and in one of the branches there was a basket. Inside was the baby. The baby was less than a month old, and that was October. I would worry about bees and insects and so on, but the mother didn't seem to care.

When we went inside she told me, "When you feed the baby, don't hold her. Leave her in the crib and put the bottle there."

I said, "Just leave the bottle and let the baby sleep in the crib?"

But that's what she told me.

And I had to get up really early in the morning. I had to make breakfast for all the children, change the diaper for the 2 year old and feed him before I went to school. There was so much work I had to do in the morning.

In the first family, Mrs. S said, "When the children get up, I want the first thing they see to be their mother." She liked to make breakfast for the children and her husband.

When I came back from school to the new place, there were no kisses, no hugs. They didn't talk to me. When I worked in the kitchen with the mother, she only told me what to do and never said a word otherwise. I was just a servant. I just worked there.

In the first family Mrs. S hired people of different cultures and different colours because they wanted the children to learn about people of different races because Canada is a multi-cultural country. She wanted the children to get to know them so they could live in harmony when they grow up.

At dinner time we all sat down and it was perfect silence. Nobody could talk at suppertime. After supper, after I cleaned up everything, we knelt down to say the rosary. The kids were so tired, and sometimes the father cheated a little bit and instead of saying the Hail Mary ten times, he would only say it six or seven times. There was no story. After this they would go to bed. They were so tired.

This is the kind of family.

The girl told her mother, "I want to tell all my classmates that we have a Chinese maid working for us. How can I prove to them that we have a Chinese maid? Can I ask Bernadette to do something that I can bring to school to show them?"

The first family told me "I love Bernadette, I love China."

Here, I don't think they were proud to have me. I think I was lower class. In Hong Kong I was well respected and the children and parents bowed and said, "Good morning, Miss Law." Here, I had to go in and out of the house by the back door. I just felt bad inside.

But I still had to keep going because I needed the money to go on.

So during the weekend they had to go out, and they told me so many times, "You have to keep an eye on the children. Don't let them fall down. Really watch them." And they said that so many times before they left the house, that I knew they didn't trust me.

When they went out on Friday night they made wieners for dinner for the children at 5 o'clock, and never told me that I could take a lunch bag or eat when I was hungry. So I had wieners for dinner.

In that place they never said I could take things from the fridge for lunch, they didn't say I could take anything. So I wasn't really happy, but I kept on doing it 7 days a week without pay, working from early morning all day, because I needed the room and board.

So one day I met the vice-principal of the school who said, "Hi, how are you managing?"

I said, "Not so good."

He asked me why, and when he found out, he took thirty dollars out of his pocket and said, "Quit the job. If you don't have money, get a student loan, and you don't have to pay it back right away, and if you score high marks you don't have to pay back the full amount."

But I didn't want to borrow money, and I didn't want to drop the job right away, but I started looking for another job because I had to make sure I had a job before I quit the last one.

I applied to the Calgary Art Centre and I got a teaching job on Saturday morning and Saturday afternoon, and I got a job teaching Oriental painting. The pay was really good: $10 for a one-hour children's class and $14 for the adults. And I applied to Continuing Education, and I got two jobs teaching painting, so I got quite good money, and I quit the babysitting job.

Mrs. Scurfield was nice. She didn't want me to stay in her place. She could have had me for four years. "But you should be on your own and enjoy your student life. You can do it." When I became a teacher, I got back my self-esteem. I really felt good. Mrs. Scurfield was very nice to me, and we still keep corresponding, because I moved to Edmonton and got a job at an Edmonton Art Gallery. I still keep in touch with that family to this day.

Mrs. Scurfield didn't go to church. Mr. Scurfield went to church, but she stayed home to make breakfast for the children. But I think she was a good Christian. The other ones said prayers and did everything the church wanted them to do, but I don't think they were very good Christians.

16. *Fay Whitehead – Grade 5*

In Grade 5, I was 10 years old, a very impressionable age. My teacher was Miss Oldfield, and she was a classical music buff. She would bring recordings of classical music, and another class would be invited to come and join us and we'd team up in these little desks and little seats, bench seats, you know, and she would play us classical music. She would explain it; she would explain the story behind the music, what it represented, and the instruments that were used, and the solo instruments she would point out what they were, and I became very conscious of music.

I had taken piano lessons for five years. My mother had wanted piano lessons and never got them, so I was the privileged one, only I didn't feel that way about it. I wanted to sing to music, or I wanted to dance to music. I didn't want to play piano, and I hated every minute of it. And finally one day I got up enough nerve to save mum the 50 cents for the teacher because I just didn't want to go.

But I kept my love of music, and I still love to dance, I can still cha-cha-cha and I'm 83.

A woman that I was friends with was a jazz enthusiast, and she taught me how to listen to jazz. It's best if you close your eyes. You can hear much better if you close your eyes.

She was trained as a concert pianist, but she was so shy she would get stage fright and she would not be able to perform, to the great disappointment of her parents.

This was in Toronto, and we would go together to the visiting jazz specialists from the States mostly, and she would want to sit in a place where she could watch the hands on the piano.

She could not play jazz. She was trained in Classical, but she was not able to switch over. It was too big a jump, and she couldn't play it, but she enjoyed it, so we would go and see Dave Brubeck and Duke Ellington. Ellington had a glass of lemon coffee – he did not drink alcohol – coffee with lemon in it. And he would have that on the table just behind him, and that was our table. We would be that close, watching him play. So I also kept my love of jazz. I still love to listen to CBC jazz in the evenings.

Other Places, Other Times

1. *Eve Baldwin – After the Air Force.*

1949 I got married to my school sweetheart and in 1952 our first boy was born. My husband was still in the Air Force. He wasn't demobbed for another year. He was stationed in England. I was living in his parents' house for the time being. When he came out of the Air Force we bought our own little flat.

Then when Patrick was six months old, I bought a mongrel dog. We called him Ching, because he had hair hanging down like a moustache. When Ching was about 8 months old, Patrick was about 9 months. My son was lying in front of the fire, which had a fireguard. One of the coals fell down and knocked the guard over and set fire to the carpet. The dog dragged my son from the living room into my bedroom to me. So of course my son and Ching were very close.

Then I had to decide whether to take Ching to Nigeria with us. My mother offered to look after him, but I said, "No! Ching is part of the family, and he has to go with us."

Well, Ching came with us and he was a very strong dog, but the Tsetse fly got him. He had at least 25 bites from the Tsetses, and he went completely blind and everything, and finally I had to give him an overdose of pentathol.

I couldn't give it to him and I had to get the Dutch doctor to give it to him because the nearest vet was 350 miles away. That was the worst choice that I have ever made, taking him to Nigeria. But Ching left lots of other little dogs in Nigeria.

He used to love to climb the rocks there and run after the bush babies. He was only a mongrel.

We were in Nigeria…I have to go by the children's ages more than anything else…we were out there in 1956.

It was an easy time there. Our boy went to the college there, though you couldn't join the college until you were 9, and he was only 8. So a teacher at the private school taught him every evening to get him up to the level so that he could get in. St. Michaels, it was called.

My daughter went to a little private school, Miss Chamberlain's School for Girls.

2. Faye Whitehead – Mexico

I fell in love with Mexico when I was ten, and we studied it in school in Grade 5 and I so admired what I learned about the people, that I decided I wanted to go there. It was in the fifties, and I was 22 when I was bridesmaid for my favourite cousin, Anita Parton, Her husband worked for Bell Telephone, and he brought home a folder one day about a tour that was being organized by Bell. She thought "Oh. Faye wants to go to Mexico." So she passed that folder on to me. And I went.

Of all the employees of Bell Telephone that went, I was the only one from the Toronto area. There were some from eastern Ontario that went, but most were from Montreal.

Being the only one from Toronto, I had to fly down to New York on my own and transfer down into the city and stay in a hotel on my own. I remember getting up early the next morning and going down to the coffee shop in the hotel and ordering orange juice, toast, and coffee.

I got the coffee. I don't know if she didn't hear me say juice and toast, but I waited politely, but it never came. And finally, when I got up enough nerve to ask, "Where's my toast and juice," she said, "Oh. Did you want toast and juice?" but it was too late, and I didn't have time.

So I got out to the airport and out to the plane. I was teamed up with another person who was travelling alone, another young woman, who I did not meet until we landed in Mexico City. Her name was Olympia Malvasio. Isn't that beautiful? She spoke English, Italian, and French, so she was very handy to have as a partner.

So we shared hotel rooms and it was a wonderfully organized tour. We saw quite a lot. We ended up with 8 days in Acapulco just lazing on the beach in a very posh hotel up on a point, so it was up where the air was moving instead of down on the beach level where it's blasting hot during the day. The temperatures dropped at night. It was very, very nice. We drove highways through mountains and desert and went to many different places. We went to a hotel spa where the swimming pool was mineral water from a waterfall. You could look up and see the waterfall. It was just wonderful. I just loved every minute of it.

And of course I met a Mexican man, and we were in correspondence when I got home. Two years later I had my 24th birthday in Mexico, meeting Roberto. He had told me that he wanted me to be his wife, but then I discovered that he was already married and had three children. So there you go.

But I did enjoy most of my stay there. It was April, and in the places I wanted to go to, like Oaxaca, it was off the tourist season and the planes weren't going there anymore. I pretty well covered a lot of the same places I went to the first time, so it wasn't terribly interesting, so I did change my flight and went home a bit early.

But then it was 24 years before I went to Mexico again with Cal, because he said, "No, we have to see Canada first."

So we went to see Canada, and then we went back to Mexico. I decided I didn't want to take him back to places I'd already been to. "Let's go someplace else. Mexico is a big country, so let's go to the Yuccatan."

So Cal fell in love with Mexico, too, and we went to several different areas, because it really is a very big country, and parts of it are very different from other parts of it, and the food is very different. They have regional cooking that's from that area only. You can have whatever you want. You can have heat and beach, or you can have height and cool. And of course all the archeological zones are fascinating. There's so much to see.

So we saw different parts of Mexico and then one year we caught a really cheap flight from Toronto to Acapulco; it was something like five days over New Year's, so we flew down there and threw away the return ticket and bused down the west coast, right down to Puerto Angel, and then we went up this wonderful country road that twisted and turned and climbed and climbed and we went through clouds, and then down the other side to Oaxaca.

We spent a month in Oaxaca, renting an apartment for $100 American. Then we went on to the Yuccatan and rented a beach house, and spent 10 winters in a row at that beach house. We never wanted to own. You can't protect the property when you're not there.

So anyway, we had our many, many visits to Mexico. We went to other places, too, other countries, but always returned to Mexico. And I will return to Mexico at least one more time to spread half of Cal's ashes off the fishing village of Chalan. And the other half will go to Stanley park.

3. Eve Baldwin— the Small Boy in Nigeria.

Small Boy was called William. He couldn't have been more than 11 years old. He followed my young daughter, who was about 2 years old. He followed her everywhere. He slept under her cot at night, and he taught her to walk, and he taught her almost to speak, really, because she was extremely lazy.

The children used to run after Baba, who was the gardener. Baba had two pails of water to water the garden, and the children would have their little bicycles, and they would go along and tip the water out of the buckets and then race on.

Well, Small Boy used to run after the children to try and stop them from tipping the pail in the first place. So there was quite a kerfuffle when this was going on.

My boy was 4 years old, and my girl was 2. They both thrived in Nigeria. But my son was more nosy, if you must say. He wanted to know everything. We were watching a group of people with Small Boy; he came with us because he wouldn't let my daughter go anywhere without him. We were watching this little band of players going along, and my son heard a sound in the bushes a few hundred yards away. He came back and said, "Mummy, the lady is having a baby."

I said. "Does she need any help?"

He runs back, "No, she doesn't need any help. It's just being born, so she's all right.

I said, "All right. Fine, thank you." He just sat down and watched it. That was a 4-year-old. He remembers bits of it. When I remind him, he says, "Oh yes, I remember that."

Of course Small Boy had to go and help the lady afterwards.

We went everywhere with Small Boy. Even in the jungle, because we were right up in the jungle. That's where we had Jane, our pet baboon

4. Eve Baldwin – Jane the Baboon

My husband found Jane tied to a tree when she was about 3 or 4 months old, and the boys were throwing stones at her, and her little insides were hanging out. She was a terrible mess.

So he brought her home to me and I put her together with gin and fishing line and she clung to my leg. I became her surrogate mother. I went dancing, played tennis, did everything with Jane on my leg.

Well, she became very heavy, and they bark like a dog, and when anyone came close she wouldn't let them near me. She was very protective. When we had to put her in her crate at night, they literally peeled her off my leg.

So we decided, "Jane's getting too big, now. We have to do something."

My husband had a friend, Mac, who lived further in the jungle. He was an entomologist, and he had four or five baboons, I'm not quite sure. So they got together, and Mack said, "Okay, I'll bring George down."

George comes down. Now Jane is very little. She never really formed properly. And George comes out of this truck. Great big massive George. And I looked at him, and I said, "Oh God, poor Jane."

Anyway, George comes over and looks at her, and she turns her head away very coyly, and he edges up to her. Well if you've seen love at first sight. It was absolutely wonderful. I could have cried, there and then. So they nudged together; he put his arm around her, and she put her hand down, ready for his hand, and it was time to go.

So Mack said, "Come on, George, we have to go, now." He had arranged that he would take Jane, but later.

George tugs Jane along into the cab with him, and I thought, "Oh, dear, she didn't even say good-bye."

But all of a sudden she jumped out of the cab, jumped on me, lathered me with all these kisses, and looked at me as if to say, "I love you, but I love George more." And off she went.

About four years later she had a young one. I am amazed because, putting her back together as I did... But we had a very happy, happy Jane in the end.

5. Karen MacGregor – Mexican Exchange Student.

I started working at 14 at what was then the Blue Sky Restaurant just on 104th Avenue behind the Tropic Isle King George. I got a couple of my friends jobs there. I went to James Ardiel Elementary School and then over to Len Shepherd High. So there was about a good half dozen of us from school working at this restaurant. It was a lot of fun.

Grade 10 brought about going to Mexico with a teacher from Len Shepherd. Neil Simm took about twenty students down. This was his fifth year doing it, taking twenty students down to Curenavaca, Mexico, about an hour southwest of Mexico City. We were billetted, two students per household, and attended classes in Spanish, continuing our studies there for two months. The afternoons and evenings were cultural exchanges, so we got to learn a lot about Mexico.

Being Canadian girls, we met Mexican boys. We started wonderful friendships down there, as the Mexican girls wanted to find out who these Canadian girls were. A blonde Canadian girl stood out a lot.

So I ended up meeting Christina. We started talking about our families: you know, how many kids in your family and that sort of thing. Our backgrounds were so similar. We were both the last child of four kids, she was learning English and her sister was learning English in England at the time.

When I got home, I had invited everybody I met down there to come back to Canada. "My parents have a big house; come on up." My parents were a little frantic that I'd invited all these Mexicans to visit.

A couple of months later, in August of 1976, my parents got a phone call. I wasn't aware of this; I was just called into the living room to talk with Mum and Dad. Well, we didn't go in the living room at that time!

They said they'd had a call from a Doctor Mallo, and he thought it would be a great experience for their daughter, Christina, to come up to Canada. To come up and learn English for a few weeks. But he wasn't just going to send his daughter up alone.

I said, "I've been working. Why don't I fly down there?" So I flew down to Mexico and stayed with the family for a couple of weeks. The three of us flew back to Canada, because Doctor Malo wasn't going to send his daughter to some place called Surrey that was somewhere on the outskirts of Vancouver.

So he came up and stayed for a couple of weeks. I attended North Surrey High School, and the dads came up to the High School and asked if she could just attend classes.

Well, there were no papers signed. The principal of the school was a member of the Kiwanis club with my Dad. Dad said to him, "I've got this Mexican girl coming and I don't know what to do with her. My wife's working, and I'm working."

He said, "Send her to school. There is no charge for an out-of-province student." There wasn't in those days.

So she came to school. She had already graduated, because she was a year older than me, so she didn't need the credits. She actually took the same typing class I did. There were only two grades there, 11 and 12. She got very well known very quickly because she was the only Mexican, and I was the Canadian girl she lived with. So during that time she stayed up for a couple of months, and she was going to fly back down again, but my parents were going down to Arizona where my grandparents had a place.

My parents said, "We'll drive her down to Arizona and we'll put her on a plane there at Christmas time." That was the plan, then.

The whole family went down to Arizona, and again I had been working. I said, "Why don't I go down to Mexico with her, and I'll fly back."

So when I got down to Mexico, I said to her Dad, "She doesn't know English that well. I think she should come back again."

Which she did. She came back with me to Canada and stayed for a few more months, and then went home.

I continued working at restaurants and went through Grade 12 in North Surrey and did an early graduation. My Dad's brother was living back in Toronto, and I decided I'd fly back to Toronto. But then it was November, and I decided to go back down to Mexico because it was getting cold.

So I ended up back down in Mexico with my Mexican family, which is still my family, still in contact with everybody down there some 40 years later. Now we have this wonderful technology. My Mexican sister is in Houston, Texas, and we talk pretty much every Sunday. We have continued this relationship.

Her father was a gastroenterologist. That's a good person to know in Mexico.

6. *Eve Baldwin – Max the Parrot.*

Where my husband worked on the transmitters in Nigeria was over 2000 feet above sea level. It was quite a climb up there. At the bottom of these mountains there was this little Nigerian woman who would sell single cigarettes and fruit or whatever, and she had this kerosene can with slits at the side, and inside was this young parrot, about three months old. My husband used to pass every day and say, "How much?"

"No sell. No sell."

One day, he said, "My last day here. I leave tomorrow. How much?"

She said, "Seven and six for the kerosene can, and three pound for the parrot."

So we bought Max. He was an African Grey. Max came home and we went to a different part of Nigeria, I think it was Ilorin. One day we were at dinner, and Max was talking wildly, really, really wildly, and I said to the boy, "What did he say?"

And the boy said, "Oh Madam, I not tell you. I not tell you."

So I said, "Okay, this is not good to hear about." So we taught him to speak English.

When our tour was finished in Nigeria, we brought him back to England, and he was speaking in my daughter's voice, you know, "Please may I get down from the table." and, "But Daddy, why do you want that?" Things like that, that you hear all the time.

In England underneath the stairs there was the gas meter, and we had the gas man come once a month to read the meter.

Max was inside in my knitting room, talking as usual, and he was saying, "Get out. Get out, I said, Get out." Which was me telling the puppies, when I was in the kitchen, to get out into the garden.

The little gas man looked at me and said, "I'm going, I'm going, it's all right. I'm going."

I said, "It's only my parrot."

He said, "Yes, madam." And off he went.

Anyway Max was quite a character. We had an evening party and the boys gave him wine. The next day Max is lying on the floor, laughing away in his little parrot fashion, and I thought "Maybe he's sick," but he couldn't get up the cage. He'd get up one or two inches and then fall back again.

Then I realized he was still drunk.

But then somebody would come to the door, and I would open the door, and he would say, "Come in, come right in. You're welcome. Come in."

People would say, "I don't want to come in."

I would say, "It's all right, it's only the parrot."

But the parrot got us into all sorts of trouble, many times. He whistled at a lady who was bending down. Then we brought him to Canada, and in Canada he was very popular with people, because he like Smarties, and we always kept Smarties on hand, so the people could give him a Smartie, and the children just loved doing this.

I used to play Scrabble with a friend, and Max used to say, "No, not B. B's wrong. B's wrong." And other Scrabble business.

When he died my friend never came after that. We could never play Scrabble after that.

He was just a wonderful bird. When he was 32 years old, he laid an egg. So I thought, "This is ridiculous." But he got egg-bound, and I couldn't find a vet, and it happened to be Easter. I even phoned the university to see if I could find a vet. Well, finally I found one but unfortunately they had to break the egg to get it away from him.

But he didn't speak for ten to twelve days afterwards. He was completely dumbstruck. He couldn't understand.

So I said to the vet, " I thought it was a 'he'."

Now, I don't know whether I believe this or not, but the vet said, "Well, If you have a coop of hens and there's no rooster, they will nominate one of the hens to become a rooster.."

And I said, "Umhum. I see. So you say my parrot just changed sex automatically just like that."

And he said, "I think so."

I'm not so sure about that. I have to find out more information on that.

He lived to be 47 years old.

7. Eve Baldwin – In Trinidad

Then we went to Trinidad in 1960 for another three years. My husband was working with Marconi, attaching the cable and wireless. That's why we went to Nigeria because Marconi offered him this job there. When that job was finished in Nigeria. He had to build the cement installation before he could install the equipment, then he had to teach the locals how to work it.

Then my husband became ill. He had caught a bug in Nigeria, the beginning of losing his lung. He became ill in Nigeria, which was why we had to leave. He got better in the three months we were going from Nigeria to Trinidad.

The doctors said he was well enough, which was wrong of them. They shouldn't have passed him as fit, but they did, and that's why we went to Trinidad. Unfortunately, in Trinidad his lung collapsed.

I had a terrible time because the white people there would phone me anonymously and say, "Get out and take your TB husband with you. Take your TB children. We don't want you here."

This was the white people. All the Trinidadian people were as loyal to me as ever. My maid wouldn't let me answer the phone. She answered the phone all the time after that. Finally the doctors said that if the children have got it, you have to go home and leave them. I couldn't do that.

Fortunately it wasn't TB at all. When we finally got back to England, the doctor said, "If you can find a nice name for a weird little bug, we'll call it that, but right now something has actually eaten the lung away."

My husband was left with one lung and he was two years in the hospital.

But he was fit to come to Canada. He went to a Harely Street doctor in London. They filled up the cavity with flesh from his spine, and made him beautifully fit. It was wonderful.

Coming to Canada, we were going to do this, and we were going to do that in Canada.

We were here in 1973, and he died in 1990. He had a good life here. The thing he did that he really wanted was to build his log cabin. But when he retired he had two years, and that was all. We had all these plans, but these things happen.

But in Trinidad they had a big park there where they have all sorts of things going on, very well known. It was called the Savannah, and many, many years afterwards, about in 1980s, I went back with a friend of mine and it was all changed.

The beautiful hotel we stayed at, it was funny. I said, "This is a wonderful hotel, and blah, blah, blah," We went there and the pool was all green with algae. I said, "Oh, that's not very good."

One woman said, "You'd better put a chair against the door when you close it."

It was a prostitutes' place. We laughed. We couldn't sleep on the bed, because it was just a sheet you could see right through.

So the next day we went into another hotel. That was an experience in itself.

8. Eve Baldwin – Lyris in Trinidad

Lyris was our maid there for all the time we were in Trinidad. She wouldn't live in our house unless she had an overnight stay to look after the children if we went out for the evening. If she had a shower, she wouldn't open the fridge for at least three hours afterwards. "You'll catch a chill."

Lyris came from a very good family. She wasn't educated, but they had money, and she had quite a lot of gold. She married this man, but she could not have children. There is a sort of unwritten law in Trinidad that if a wife cannot produce children, the husband is allowed to find a woman who can. So he found a young woman, and they had two or three children.

And all this had to be paid for by Lyris, who kept pawning her gold pieces to get the money. It wasn't a double marriage. He was married to Lyris, but the other woman had the children, and Lyris paid for it.

Lyris got tired of this, and she had no gold left. We happened to be there at that time, and she offered to become my maid. She'd never done this work before, but she was a lovely person.

She had six fingers on each hand. The sixth finger actually worked. My children used to be very fascinated by this. They used to say, "Use your sixth finger, Lyris, use your sixth finger."

Anyway, Lyris came to work for us to get the money to get her gold out of pawn. Which she did. She finally got her gold back because Bob's company paid her quite well. Then she said, "I not stay marry him."

I said, "Well, can you get a divorce?"

Between my husband and another friend of hers she finally got the divorce.

She was very devoted to my husband. My mother used to send me a terrible perfume from Devonshire called "Devon Violet." She only sent it to remind me of England and for the little vials it came in. So I used to say, "Here you are, Lyris."

So Lyris would wear this heavy perfume and serve us dinner. My husband would turn to her and say, "You smell lovely tonight, Lyris."

She would sort of bend her head and say, "Thank you, Master."

She was a very devoted servant. When my husband was in hospital there, I had a little open car like an MG, a red one. She would have her shower and dress up in her beautiful uniform and sit in the front seat and smile at the other maids, and say, "I'm going to see my master." She was just a wonderful person.

When we left she didn't work again. She did become a nursemaid for two little children

For ages afterwards we kept in touch. I had a picture of her with the children. Then she got Alzheimer's. I went to Trinidad after that on a cruise, and I went to the home to see her, and she didn't know me at first. Then she said, "Ah! Madam!" and then it was gone. Just for that one moment it was there, then it was gone.

She died soon after, and I was so glad I went to see her, because for just that one moment she knew me. She said, "Ah! Madam!" and then she was gone.

She was a beautiful person.

9. Eve Baldwin – Grouse for Dinner

I was having people for dinner. There were only about four families there, but of course we all got together. I thought it was my turn to do dinner, so I went down to the market and grabbed some birds, sort of like grouse. You bought them alive, you know. So I bought two of these and put them in the trunk of the car.

When I got back to my house, I said to the boys, "The birds are in the back of the car."

They opened the trunk and the birds flew. They flew up into these big trees, right in the middle of the jungle. So I thought the only thing to do was to get the rifle. So I got the rifle and I went out and I tried to shoot them. One of them dropped, but the other one stayed up there.

My husband came home, and I said, "If you want dinner, it's up in the tree."

He took the pellet gun, but to this day the stupid bird is still up in the tree, because we never got it down.

That was just the kind of thing that happened. But the people came over and we made do with what we had.

10. Eve Baldwin – Red nails at the Market

I had my nails painted red, and I was walking with the two children. My son was about five years old, and all of a sudden he calls, "Vultures, Mummy. It's the vultures!"

The vultures were swarming around, thinking my red toes were meat. They were all flocking, about four or five of them were suddenly flocking around me.

One of the men who was working there took off his little shawl thing and put it around my feet, and I shuffled my way out of the market with this shawl around my feet.

I never, ever painted my nails red again to go to the market.

11. Karen MacGregor – Camping in Mexico

My trip was from Toronto to Mexico City. I was picked up by my Mexican parents there. My brothers and sisters down there had already left to go camping at the beach for the weekend. I'm used to camping here, going to Cultus, but camping down there was a little bit different. So we left Mexico City, an hour to Cuernavaca where I was picked up by another friend. Then we drove through another state into Acapulco state.

At these border crossings you have the military. A little shocking to have somebody very close to my same age pointing a rifle at me. This does not happen in Canada when we go camping. Understanding that that in Guererro state, Acapulco at that time was a big drug crossing, so we were getting checked out going through. Now I'm the Canadian going across. "Okay, shake hands, they love the Canadians." Sadly for my American friends, the Canadians were greeted with big smiles and "What's it like up there?"

Then we got to Acapulco, and I thought we were going to stay, and I remembered the stories and movies I'd seen about Acapulco. But we weren't staying in Acapulco. We were actually driving through the jungle. The road was more like a pathway for a donkey to go through, very rough, hot, humid. Down to Copala, about three hours south of Acapulco.

When we got there it was not a five-star hotel. It was a "find your spot on the beach." We got there about mid-November 1978, I guess. It was very primitive. These were people who lived on the beach. A lot of them were of African-Mexican descent. There I am, and you could spot me, because I'm the white girl. Really white and blonde.

But the amazing things that I got to see. Being on the beach and the open ocean, they warned me. They said, "It's open ocean. There's sharks. Don't go out too far." I'm a very strong swimmer, but I'm glad I heeded what they said.

The first day, all I could remember hearing was "Cuidado, cuidado." Which was "Be careful, be careful."

So, not really getting it, but the next morning I wake up and my face was puffed out from being totally fried. I had to stay out of the sun that day. The little kids that were there, this was pretty scary for them to see this person. My cheeks puffed as far out as my nose. I looked Asian with my slitted eyes. Thank goodness it didn't do any permanent damage. Back then we suntanned. We put on baby oil. That was the 70s. All I kept thinking was, "Man, this is going to be a good tan, later.

But to stay there and be on the beach and witness tortoises coming up in the morning. The big treat was we were going to have eggs for breakfast. I wasn't very environmentally aware back then, and I ate tortoise eggs. But also we watched some of the tortoises burying the eggs in the sand and going back to the ocean. That experience is embedded in my mind. It was awesome.

Also a huge wave coming up and washing all these fish up onto the shore. All the people that lived there came rushing down and gathered up all these fish. It was one of those rogue waves. That's what we ate. Oysters right out of the ocean, cracked open. There was no "Food Safe" but we survived. We drank beer. We didn't drink the water.

There were no shops there. We're talking people who would come out on horseback to sell bread to us. A thunderstorm on the open ocean and the rain pelting down. Lightening up the sky so much. We were in those old canvas tents. You didn't sleep in; it was so stinking hot by the time the morning rolled round. And there were no public washrooms, either. It was, "You want me to go just around the corner?" I can say we all ended up being a little anal retentive at that point.

That experience. I got to go to Copala a couple of times. That trip was fabulous because Christina's boyfriend at the time, his father flew a small plane. He landed it on the beach. These things don't happen in Canada.

Because I was so burnt and because it was at least a 6-hour drive back to Cuernavaca, I was able to fly back with him. Again, there I am up in this plane, and I'm thinking, "Mum, Dad, if you knew where I was right now, you wouldn't believe it."

That was quite a trip.

Another trip that I went on as well, we had travelled back there again, this was a couple of years later, so I knew the routine, but when we left we decided we would come back at night. We would leave at like one in the morning because it's cooler.

One of the friends we were with had a horrible earache, and he was lying in the back seat. As we came across the border again with all the guys with rifles and things like this, we were stalled for a very long time. They were suspicious. I didn't have my passport with me.

A couple of my girlfriends had flown down, too. They were already across the border, but we're stalled. They're only 5 yards ahead of us sitting on the back of the pickup truck having a cold beer with the driver.

I don't know what happens, but Pepe gets off his truck with Sergio. They come running back. I understood Spanish, but I really didn't catch what was going on. The next thing I know, everybody's saluting everybody, we're in the car and we're off.

We get across the border, and I'm looking back at these guys, and "What the heck happened there?"

Well, I guess Pepe's Dad was a general in the army. That's the way it's done there. And luckily the people that I knew, knew people. We weren't doing anything wrong, but I remember sitting in the back of the car thinking, "Geez, I'm only 18. It was a good life. I did a lot of things, but I guess this is it." I really didn't know how, but because of the forces and the connections, we were okay, so back to Cuernavaca we went.

Norm: I might interject that this is the first time I'm hearing this story.

Karen: Yeah, I held off on this one. I still have a sixteen-year-old, so I'm not quite telling these stories yet. I guess that one will come out in the book, won't it?

I have had a gun pointed at my head a couple of times, and it's very scary. You learn to be respectful, there. It was quite exciting. Exhilliarating at the time.

12. Karen MacGregor – Knowing People

Another friend had come down to Mexico to visit, and as we were putting her on a plane back to Canada, we drove her to the airport in Mexico City. Again, through people that we knew, somehow we were in the office of the general manager of the airport having a drink with him. My sister, Susannah was with us, and we're having a chat, and it's time for Debbie to board the plane, and they invite me onto the plane as well. So I'm sitting there on the plane as everyone else is boarding. I meet the pilots, up into the cockpit.

The security was pretty relaxed in 1979 when you knew people. One of the cousins worked at the airport. When I was going through the airport coming down to Mexico, just by fluke I went to get my bags, and he saw me and just whipped me right through.

A couple of times I went down two or three times a year. I was working and travelling, having fun experiences. And it's funny all these years later being back here. I always missed the plazas in the towns. If there was nothing going on you just went down to the plaza and had a coffee or whatever. And now I'm so happy to see that happening in Surrey with the city hall and the plazas. We're creating this downtown core that people can come to.

13. Joan Campbell – Living in South Africa

We immigrated to Johannesburg after the War, with just one child, and the first day I walked down the road on my own and my husband was watching our daughter. I walked down the road, and by the time I got down to the bottom of the road I knew what it was all about, because I only saw two other white faces, and all the rest were the real African people. I thought. "Oh. Now I understand a bit what this country's all about." There were ten coloureds to two of the white, and the white wanted to be in charge, of course. They had the power.

I went back to the house and I said, "Now I understand what kind of a country we've come to."

And Pat was taking me back to a country he knew. His claim to fame: he was the first white Coca Cola salesman in Capetown. He was the first white selling Coca Cola. That poisonous stuff. You can clean rust off with that.

We stayed there after the War. Everywhere had problems, terrible times. People coming home. The women had to get out of the factories. The men coming home had to have the jobs, and the women had their independence and they were starting to flex their muscles.

So we stayed there for three to four years. We had our second daughter, Sue, there. Annie was born in Germany after the War. But I never had a Canadian son. We always wanted a Canadian son. The third girl, you know, she was born, and, "Here I am! Notice me!" She was more like boy.

We rented a place out in the country.. Johnnie was our boy: the cook, the everything boy. He had his own personal hut outside our house. Our house was very plain, with no electricity.

I walked through the black township the first day. I pushed the chair because I wanted something from the pharmacy, and there was a pharmacy in the black township. So I pushed the one-year-old in the pram, and I was very interested in seeing everything. I noticed homes, some very dilapidated. I walked through, got a white pharmacist, and walked back.

My neighbor said, "Where have you been?"

I said, "I've just been up to the township."

She gasped. "You don't do that," she says. "You don't do that."

You see, I showed no fear, and they respected a mother with a child. I showed no fear on my face. I walked through, looking around, very interested, looking around, a smile on my face, saying "Hello, good morning," to everyone.

I went one more time after this, but then, of course, it was dangerous. But I knew if I had no fear I would be all right, and I really needed something. But my neighbor was horrified. So she started to tell me. Her husband was a brain surgeon, and she'd only lived in Africa. You'd go to her place and she'd say, "Oh, George, porte le the," she'd say, and give out orders, and he was a lovely older black man. He would bring the tea and so she'd tell me how we had to act. She said, "You lock up your coffee, tea, and sugar. You give Johnnie enough for the day." Well, of course we laughed about this. We were ignorant immigrants.

We thought, "That's terrible."

Well, how many years later he went off back to Swaziland and bought another life. My mother was staying with me, and she said, "It's funny, Johnnie had a big case that he took with him. A big case." And Pat and I looked at each other. "Coffee, tea and sugar."

Every night he would help himself to a cup and store it. It makes sense. We understood perfectly. But we realized we had to listen to our neighbors when they told us how we had to act.

Johnnie had a place with us. We were his family, and he said, "Terrible place. Madame," He was Johnnie, and the girls loved him. He had his children. With a cow he bought a wife. When he went back home with a cow he came back with a wife. He was a father. He had children, lots of children, of course.

There were three levels in their society. There were the Africans, the Afrikaans, and the British. And you didn't talk politics. Especially when it got closer to apartheid.

When we left, we all cried. My husband didn't, but he was driving. We were waving to Johnnie, and he had tears streaming down, and the children were crying and I was crying – what a bunch – because we were leaving Johnnie behind.

But that was after years. And then we went back to Canada and went to the Arctic.

In the Military

1. Tom Brown — *The Experience of Battle*

When I arrived in Peterborough for basic training, I thought at that time I was just going to stay in reserve. When you got called up you didn't have to go overseas, you could stay in Canada.

But I wanted to be a mechanic. When I was in training they'd allow us to take the machines apart and run them. They had no end of tools. I realized, "Boy, I can do well, here."

But still, I don't know why I did it. I guess it must have been that I could get more training by going overseas. But I went over there. It was an experience I don't talk about much.

You have to put it away. If you start thinking there, that's what gets you in trouble, if you start going back. It was a long time ago. I went in with the invasion, and I was there when the war ended. That was a year and a half about.

I was never in a house or anything; it was just outdoors and in the tanks. It's a bad thing, because you're responsible for the crew, and you get out there at night and you don't want to get lost out there. It's the easiest thing in the world in the dark. If you get turned around and going the wrong way, you're pointin' back at your own guys. The same thing with the other people, running around out there. You got your job to do and you have to do it.

So there's a lot of things that go on, and so then if you start thinking back about things, it can get you. You just didn't allow yourself to think or talk about it for years. Later, maybe 40 years, it didn't seem to be too bad.

But the thing is, from the invasion, that's the first time I realized that I made a big mistake. We were going over in the landing barges. Before, in England, they'd load us up, take us around the harbour, then land us on shore; that was okay. But the real thing was different.

At daybreak the sky was just full of bombers coming as far as you could see, and the battleships were lined up there and then we started hearing them firing. And then you think, "This is a big deal." But then you get closer, and the shells started coming from shore, and that's the last I remember, really, until that first big town there, I forget what it's called, now.

I can't recall that, again, but we were in the town, and they called us back. It was kind of a mountain up high, at night, and then in the morning, again, that was a big raid, and boy, they just flattened that city, I remember watching, so there's certain things like that stay with you, but otherwise...

It was the same thing in the tank work. At night, you could either dig a slit trench or get in one the Germans had left and stay there. That was the safest place, though with the shells coming in you'd get covered in mud and stuff. Except if you were in trees. That was really bad. The shell would hit the trees and then down it comes on top of you. Anything that the shells could hit and explode.

Sometimes you'd get careless, you know, you'd get tired and heck, rather than having to dig one yourself, you'd say, "I'll take a chance." That wasn't a good idea.

Next day you get up and get in the tank and go.

One thing Hitler did on the Invasion, there. What they found out with the land mines. When you step on them they'd get one person, maybe. But he decided to make a deal where the mines you stepped on it there was a small charge would shoot the land mine up about six or eight feet in the air and explode and get everybody.

That's the war part. Again, we didn't see more than a little of it. We didn't know what was going on. We didn't see more than our little deal. But that was a year and a half, I guess, I was never in a house... Well I shouldn't say never, because there were bombed out houses, and we'd get in there but I don't think we ever slept in there because it wasn't safe. So you were never in a house. We never had white bread until we were up in Niemegen the first winter, when they had a little store, there. We had dry rations and that was it.

So I don't remember too much of what went on in the war.

2. Joan Campbell – War Bride.

I met my husband through my brother in Chelsey, Battersea in London during the war. My brother said, "I've met this interesting Canadian. He has the most incredible stories to tell about South Africa. That's where he was before the War. I want you to meet this fascinating fellow, Joan."

Well, I was fascinated. He was a real charmer. He said he was out in the bush. That's a very strange expression. In England, you don't talk about being out in the bush. He was a sergeant in the RCA Service Corps when I met him.

I was in an apartment in the basement. When I met him I was in my first job, and I was in a basement, and I paid a pound a week in rent. You went down the steps because it was below pavement. I was really happy. I was earning money for the first time, and very proud of myself. So when I met him, he was out in the bush, and he would write to me, and I would wait every morning and I'd hear, "plop," when the postman came down and pushed it through the letterbox. And I'd hear "plop," and it was my letter from Pat, my boyfriend. And there would be the letter for me. He would write about what he was doing in the bush. They were in training, in maneuvers. That would be before 1942, I suppose. I get dates and everything mixed up.

Pat's brother told him, "If you're serious about this English girl, you should go back and get your officer's qualifications." I liked him as he was. I was quite happy with him.

So he went back, so we did have quite a long time. But the romantic point; New Year's Eve there were bombs dropping and everything. Just as New Years' was coming we went up on the roof, which you shouldn't do, of course, but we did. We went up on the roof and there were flashing lights and sirens going on, and we had drinks, of course. We were quite merry. And he said, "Will you marry me? This year or next year, whenever the right time is." That was very romantic.

For our honeymoon, we went to a theatre in London, and there was a raid, and nobody took any notice. It was a time to have fun. Especially when the men were going off, and you didn't know what would happen to them. On our honeymoon we went to the theatre, and there was an air raid warning, and nobody took any notice, and the chandeliers in this old theatre were shaking from the bombs dropping, not on us, but close enough, and nobody took any notice at all. Isn't it amazing? We were both in our own seventh heaven. We were happy.

We did spend a honeymoon, a few days, in one of the bigger hotels in London. It made you feel fairly safe.

But he got a telegram the next day. Day two of our honeymoon, he got a telegram and I got a telegram, too. He had to report for duty. It was D-Day plus some, and he had to return to his unit right away. I got a telegram, and a new lot of wounded came in, and we had to get back to work. I was in a rehab place. So we didn't have a proper honeymoon.

Within three weeks he was wounded. It was ironic, because it was D-Day plus about 13, and he said he felt as though a table had come and banged into his shoulder. He fell on the floor. Everything was so well organized. He was leading his platoon. If anyone fell, the ambulance came right up, wherever they'd fallen, whipped him back. His sergeant took over his platoon and he was killed at the next river crossing. Pat felt very guilty. He talked to me about it several times, but he had terrible guilt feelings. He was wounded at the back of his arm, and it cut a nerve, and he had to go straight to England.

In three weeks he was back in England with his arm in a sling. He looked terrible. The noise of the guns, in three weeks he was gaunt. He'd lost weight and looked terrible.

I was in a job out in Hitchin. I went out to work every day, and he stayed in my boarding house with me. But he went up to London every day to say, "When do I go back?" He wanted to go back. He felt if he didn't go back, he wouldn't want to go back.

He went back and had incredible experiences. But the British officers were falling like flies, so he went back allocated to the Canloan program, and he was given a platoon of Glasgow guys, little toughies. They'd been in the war several years, and they were bloody sick of it. They were sick and ready to get out. I watched our lads. It was the same with the Germans. They didn't care who won; they just wanted to get out. They'd seen horrors. Friends mown down, dying.

So he had to urge these men on, to go forward, and they'd had enough. They were tough, and they fought, but towards the end of the war, they wanted the war to end, and you could understand. There was no romance at all.

In those days I was very serious about my life. I've got lighter and more silly and naughty as I have aged. Women do, actually. Men get more mellow, generally. I've read this. It's not just me. People say that when the men get over their hormones that put everything into the one part of their body, then they gradually settle down and begin to value the women for their worth, hopefully. It is improving. Look at the Canadian women, Rah, rah, rah. And then the women get more relaxed and free. They've had their children and they enjoy the grandchildren. You enjoy them more as you get older

It's funny, though, during the war when we had dances, when the men were on leave, it wasn't the officers the women were looking for. We had boyfriends or husbands, but we would dance with people, and we wanted the non-commissioned men. We found those men more interesting. We were all discussing them, "Oh, I like that one, no not that one." They were more down-to-earth. They were the ones we wanted to dance with. They were just having some fun.

It was another life.

3. Eve Baldwin – Air Force and Bletchley Park

I was 17 when I finished school. I didn't know what to do.

I wanted to be a vet very badly, and I went to university in Bristol, and my professor there said, "Evelyn, you'll never be a vet. Your theory is good, but your practical…"

I couldn't put a needle in an animal to put it to sleep. I cried when a woman brought a little cat in to be put down. The vet I used to work with on Saturday morning said, "You can't do this."

And I said, "No, I can't."

I thought, "Instead I'll join the Air Force. I'll go kill Hitler or something."

I forged my father's name because I wasn't 18 yet, and my father thought I was still at school. I used to send letters to my friend at school and she used to forward them on to him.

Towards the end of 1943, I was getting kind of bored with the job I was doing in the Gloucester Records Department. I heard from a friend that there was a Code and Cypher department. I had done a lot of secret codes with my father, very childish codes. We used to leave coded messages for each other. Just letter substitutions and that. I thought, "Why can't I go in for that?" Well, I applied for Code and Cypher, and I was going to go for training when I found myself having an interview to go to Bletchley Park.

I didn't know what it was for, they just told me that there would be an opening there for me. I went along and met an officer at Bletchley. He told me that before he could say anything I had to obey this thick Secret Codes Act for 99 years. Before they even interviewed me I had to sign it, so I wouldn't tell anybody that I had seen anything. Not that I had.

I was interested in the building. It was a beautiful big mansion, a spectacular place. They told me that they needed a girl. The WAFs weren't there to begin with. It was originally the WRENs. They were the ones doing the decoding. They were Navy. Then they called in a few Army, then the Air Force, and that was us.

And there was me. I have no idea why they chose me. I happened to mention childish codes between my father and myself, and that evidently ticked something in their minds. I had a great time, but it was a boring job. I was just passing messages. People would put their hand up with a message in it. I would take it and read what department or what hut I was to take it to, and I just took it.

I wasn't allowed to read it or anything, I just took it.

We were just clerks, doing clerical work there. I'm very proud of it now, but at the time it was just a job. It was just a classified job we were doing.

We used to do the grids of crosswords, and the boffins used to do all the solutions and the questions for the crosswords. That was when we had a few minutes

Ian Fleming was there. He was an Army officer. I didn't know he was going to be famous. If I'd known, I'd have got his autograph.

Fun times.

I didn't tell my husband I had been at Bletchley until 1986 when I got a letter saying that the secret code act was abolished.

So I told my husband, and he said, "I can't believe it."

It was a secret for all of us, and all our lives it will be a secret somehow or other. When you sign something like that, you sign it for life. Not just for a period of time. Even when they tell you it's okay, you wouldn't breathe a word of it.

I was there for about a year, and then in the end of 1944, around about Christmas, they said that I was going to India. I had lived in India, and they wanted information from different people that my father knew. So I went to India.

But I still hadn't told my father that I was in the Air Force. I couldn't tell him I was at Bletchley; I wasn't allowed to tell him anything. He still thought I was at school. In the meantime he had joined the Naval Reserve.

I was on the ship going to India and who was inspecting the ship but my father.

He saw me in line there and he took a second look and he couldn't believe his eyes, and I couldn't believe mine. He just came up to me and said, "Go to the captain's cabin."

So I very shyly went. "He's going to tell me to go home," and I was in tears and everything.

He said, "I don't mind you joining and fighting in the war. But why the Air Force?"

I sad, "Dad, they only wanted cooks in the Navy. And you know what I'm like in the kitchen. The only thing I make that has to do with food is reservations."

He got over it, but what hurt him most was the slyness. I did it without him knowing, which was very bad. I shouldn't have done that. And for that length of time. I should have had more trust in him.

In any case I couldn't tell him I was at Bletchley.

I went to India then, because they knew that I had contacts in India, and I spoke Hindi.

It wasn't very much. I had a few meetings with Dr. Humdahni and Mamaji, who were my father's friends. He was still in contact with them. I was there a short while, maybe six months, and then I was off to Singapore. I guess I did what I was supposed to do, and they just posted me here and there. I didn't mind, because I liked the change. I loved India.

4. Eve Baldwin – Singapore

Then a Singapore posting came. I went to Singapore just as the remaining Japanese were leaving. They wanted to find if it was suitable for the WAF to go there, if it was a suitable place.

When we went there the Japanese had taken over a big, almost like a castle with a moat around it, and that's where the soldiers were sleeping. The officers had a special row of little houses.

When I went there the Japanese were still leaving, and we literally had to wash the floors before we could put our palettes down for sleeping. As they came out, we went in.

I can't describe what it was like. It was a dirty, filthy mess. But we cleaned it all up. We laughed and joked and cleaned it all up. There were only about half a dozen of us.

We were actually housed in what was the Japanese married quarters, a terrace of six or eight houses, two stories. I shared that with my friend.

I had just got my commission. So I was very junior. I was an Assistant Section Officer, very junior. The bottom. So I was sharing with another officer of the same rank. The senior officers had a house of their own, of course.

Then they covered up the moat. It had a drawbridge and everything. I loved it. I was sorry that they covered in the moat. But they did, and took the drawbridge away. Then the WAFs came out, and we officers were given the little houses.

On our caps we had this shiny badge, and one morning I was on duty at ten or eleven o'clockand I couldn't find it.

I was searching everywhere. Suddenly a heard a ruckus outside. A lot of noise and scraping and squeaking. I looked outside, and there was a ring of monkeys. They had my hat, and they were throwing it to each other.

I thought, "How on earth am I going to get my hat back?"

There was this Japanese boy, a prisoner of war. They were being used to work the grounds. Usually they were chained or roped together, but this boy was on his own. He couldn't have been more than 17 or 18. He went into the middle of the monkeys, and he took a papaya and he threw it in the middle. The monkeys went for it, and the hat gradually got out.

The boy got the hat and gave it to me with a big bow.

I thanked him.

Several mornings after that, it would be a little bunch of wild flowers or grasses on my mat.

One day he knocked on my door, which was very unusual. I knew that he was leaving. There were about twenty of them left, and they were being repatriated.

In his Japanese he said that he was going. From his neck he took a chain. It was really moldy. It was green and moldy, but he took it from his neck and put it in my hand.

When I looked at it afterwards it was a medallion of the Madonna. So he was Roman Catholic. I had it cleaned and years later I met one of the officers who was out there, and I asked him if he could find out anything about this boy.

Finally it came around that these Japanese were not full Japanese, but had either a Japanese mother or a Japanese father, and evidently in the case of this boy, a Catholic. So I had this little chain and this medallion, and I put it on my charm bracelet, which somebody very kindly stole from me. I had all sorts of beautiful things on it. I had it all those years, and it was stolen here, in Surrey.

He was an exceptional Japanese boy.

I was there from the end of 44 to 47. I was demobbed from Singapore in 1948. My tour was up and most of the people were demobbed unless you wanted to stay on. I didn't want to stay on. I had done my 6 years in the Air Force. That was enough.

I was going to get married anyway.

5. John Palen – Air Force

Three other boys and myself went down to the recruitment depot and joined the Air Force. I was 19, and the other boys were roughly the same age.

I chose the Air Force because as high school students we knew that everybody was going to be recruited, and you'd have no choice. During the Twenties when I grew up, I was very interested in airplanes. They were the thing of the future.

I had a book all about Billy Bishop from the First World War, and so there was no other thought in my mind. We weren't interested in marching around, so we joined the Air Force instead of the Army.

Once I joined the Air Force I was stationed at the Manning Depot at the Exhibition Grounds in Toronto. If you joined the Navy they had a separate building for Navy personnel, and another building for Army personnel. From there I went to Montjoli Quebec, to the Number 9 gunnery to learn to be a tail gunner. It was just to the east of Quebec City, and there we learned Morse Code and the operation of guns and turrets and everything. We used to fly in simulated battles up and down the St Lawrence River. That was where we got some aerial training.

I graduated from there in July 1943 and then I was put on an embarkation leave, because I was going overseas. I was sent to Halifax for one week, and then I was called out on a draft, and we were marched down towards the docks. I thought we were getting an ocean liner, and we got down to the docks and we marched through a big shed. On the other side of the shed was a train. We got on the train and crossed the border into New York and Vermont and that and went all the way down to New York City. We caught an ocean liner there.

There was a heat wave in New York. God, it was hot.

We were put on this ship with thousands of American troops. We crossed the Atlantic Ocean. I made a fatal mistake because I picked a top bunk, and it was so damned hot up there. Of course the water fountains were not on all the time, and you had to ration your bottle of water. There were 10 men in a normal state room where in most times it would be for a couple. We had six bunks and four guys slept on the floor. They had the coolest spot.

We eventually reached land. One morning the ship anchored, and there were seagulls flying around. There was kind of a drizzle and the big barges came up out of this bay we were in. We got on board the barges. We still didn't know where we were. But as we went down the bay further we could hear bagpipes. So we got the message. We were in Scotland

Then we got on a train and went down to Bournemouth, England. I only stayed there for 10 days, and then I was called out on a draft, and I was sent up to Kinloss, Scotland. I had arrived in Scotland, come all the way down to the south coast of England, and before two weeks were up I was back to Scotland.

It was an air base at Kinloss. There were ten of us or so sent up. We got in there and that's where we got crewed up with an English crew. We were with the Royal Air Force on an English bomber, and like a lot of Canadian boys that went overseas I got put into an English squadron.

That's where I met my different crew members. The crew consisted of a pilot, navigator, flight engineer, wireless operator, mid-uppergunner, and tailgunner. Seven of us.

We did training there for two or three months because keep in mind, this was a new experience, flying in a Whitley bomber, a two-engine type. They weren't used in Bomber Command any more, so they used them in training, to give the pilot practice at flying and takeoffs and landings, and the other crew members used to their particular positions.

After two or three months we were all finished, but our navigator unfortunately got appendicitis and went into the hospital and had his appendix out.

We had only one more night trip to do, so we took a spare navigator and got our trip in. Then he came out of the hospital, and he had to get his night trip in, so he flew with this other crew and they unfortunately ran into a German night fighter over Northern England and they were shot down and all of them killed.

So here we were. We thought, "To get a new navigator, we'll have to take the whole course over again!"

But there was a navigational instructor at Kinloss who had done a tour already in the Middle East on Wellingtons. He wanted to come back, and he heard of our predicament.

"If you guys like," he says, "I'll come as your navigator."

We said, "Welcome!"

I've often said that was the best break we ever got, because in a lot of planes the navigators weren't experienced. They graduated from their navigation class in Canada under the British Training Program, but when the got up in the air over Germany and had to do their navigation...if they made any errors and gave the pilot the wrong course, it could cause a lot of problems.

So that was a great break.

Eventually we finished there and we went to another station to get onto Halifax bombers, the four-engine ones.

Then we trained on the Halifaxes for a month, getting used to the equipment there, with the pilot getting more training in takeoffs and landings, because flying a four-engine bomber was a lot different from flying a two-engine one.

Then we were posted to 77 Squadron Alvington, Yorkshire, located roughly 10 miles south of the city of York. And if you know your English history, you know that York was a very historic city. The Romans had quite a place, there.

From there we started doing operations. Our first trip was in December 1943, to the big city of Berlin. It was quite a trip.

6. *John Palen – The Pathfinders.*

The Pathfinders used to travel around to all the squadrons looking for new recruits to go to the Pathfinders. They were the ones who led the raid and did the marking for the targets for the main force of bombers. They still used a full-sized bomber, but they had these extra duties.

That was another thing. When you joined the Pathfinders you had to guarantee you would do two tours. Normally in bomber command you only did one tour. But you had to do two tours in the Pathfinders. But that made a lot of crews think about it. Especially a lot of the English boys, who were married and had families. Most of the crews, once they did their tour, they would be assigned to somewhere as an instructor or other ground crew.

As a crew, each person had a say if we all wanted to go and join the Pathfinders. Around April of 1944, we said, "Why not? They get all the best of the equipment." So we joined the Pathfinders. We were put on 635 Pathfinders Squadron, on the East Coast of England right near King's Lynne. That's where Lord Nelson was born.

We did another 30 trips from there. We did 18 trips in the Halifax at the other squadron. So we did 48 trips altogether.

Sometimes the Master Bomber would fly a Mosquito, a two-engine bomber. Once the target was identified the Master Bomber would open the attack by dropping a floating flare. For our first few trips we went in with the Master Bomber to give him support. The Master Bomber had to stay around the target area for the whole time to make sure the flares were coming down in the right spot. It's his responsibility if the flares are off to give instructions over the wireless for the other planes. Keep in mind on a big raid you can have six, seven, eight hundred planes and the whole raid could last an hour over the target.

In the Pathfinders you were assigned a very specific time you were to drop your markers. The Pathfinder might go in first, or you might be assigned to the tail end. These are special marking flares that only burn for maybe 10 minutes, so you have to refresh them.

You had to make sure that you were getting your flares down in the right spot. They had different types of flares. If the target area was covered in cloud, it had to be identified by radar.

Our last trip was to Ulm, the birthplace of Einstein. We were on our way home, and we were told over the radio from our commander at the station saying, "Okay, boys, this was your last trip. You're all through."

We were all through, but also keep in mind that over the last year we were very close together as a crew. We had become a unit, working together and we were very close socially. When I got back I was sent home to Canada, but I kept in touch with the various boys over the years, and as far as I know, I think I'm the only one still living. I know our pilot got a job with one of the British Airlines. The Navigator flew with BOAC, London to New York for 25 years. Then they did away with navigators because they had all the modern equipment. So he went to Australia and flew with Quantas from Sidney to Los Angeles on the Pacific Run because they needed navigators for that long trip.

I kept in touch with them at Christmas with cards. The mid-upper gunner died just a couple of years ago. But I don't know what the story is on any of the others.

So I came home.

7. John Palen – D-Day

On the night of June 5 we were told that we were on duty, and we went for a briefing. At the briefing all they mentioned was that there was a large armada crossing the English Channel and we were going to go out and bomb some of the big gun emplacements on the French Coast. We were briefed and we had our last supper and everything but when we went out to the plane we had a glycol leak in one of the engines, so we couldn't take off, and there was no spare plane, so we missed out on that.

But we were out the next day anyway. At our briefing that night they had some leaflets that anybody could pick up. I'm a collector of leaflets, if they have historic significance. Even then, I was thinking, "D-Day, that's a historic day." So I brought one of those home. It was a letter from General Eisenhower, the Commander-in-Chief. And I kept it for years and years in good shape. I made a few copies, and I gave the original copy to the Museum in Camp Borden.

During the next month after D-Day we were bombing a lot of marshalling yards, railway stations and oil depots in France, Belgium, Holland. It was tactical bombing. Anything that would help the troops work their way in. You weren't running into a lot of fighters. Although some of those French targets we were on, we lost maybe 15 or 20 planes every night to German fighters.

A Full Life

Editor's Note: Norm Schmidt opened the first Optometry clinic in Surrey in the 1950s, and has been very active in the community there ever since. He and his daughter, Karen MacGregor, had a fine time telling each other stories, some of which the other had never heard before!

1. Norm Schmidt– Early Life.

I was raised in Kerrisdale. It all started when I was born in 1930 in the depths of the depression. The market crash had happened a couple of months before I was born. My Dad suggested to me that maybe I was the cause of it. My Dad was a teacher at Kitsilano High School.

It was propitious that I attend where my Dad taught so he could keep an eye on me. It was not a happy time for me, because I had a lot of extracurricular activities that my Dad did not appreciate me being involved with.

I ran a class newspaper. That was fun. One of my friends had a hectograph. It's a device that makes maybe 50 copies. This was before Gestetner came on line. I ran into problems with the teachers. They did not like my political content.

I knew all these teachers personally. I knew their first names, their drinking habits. I made reference to these at times. That is when the teachers suddenly took an interest in this publication. I think I stepped over the line a bit. There are teachers with drinking habits. In fact, having kids like me in class...

Other than that I just did the usual school things. I wasn't active in sports. I was more of the literary type. One of the few skills I came out of high school with; to fill up my grade 12 electives, "Oh! I'll take typing!"

One thing I wish I had also taken was shorthand. At UBC if you skipped class you could always get somebody else's notes. But if you knew shorthand, nobody could read them.

I was in the big crush of classes. The great number of DVA people coming out of the war got well paid. The population of UBC had spiraled up to something like seven or eight thousand. I was on the down side. I understand today UBC has something like 30,000 students. It's big business everywhere.

My parents had a summer vacation home at Gibsons. That was way out in the woods. The Union Steamship line was active at that time. I spent my summers there, bare from the waist up. By the time I'd get back too school, people would say, "Oh, you have such a healthy looking tan." Nobody ever told usthat it would give us skin cancer later on.

One of my Dad's hobbies was fishing. And smoking. Not necessarily in that order. But there was no power available at Gibsons in those days, and if we came home with three nice Spring salmon, we had to eat the damn things. Either that, or, "Norm, go down to the Co-op and get another dozen glass jars. We'll can them."

And that led to, "Norm go down to the beach and get firewood." And in the heat of August we would be in the kitchen canning. Terrible thing, keeping that fire going.

Later the Black Ball Ferry came into existence with that run but it was going to cost $2 for an adult to go from Vancouver to Gibsons. My Dad, in a fit of anger, said, "I'm not going to pay that. That's highway robbery." Today it would be 20 bucks, I'm sure.

Our place was on Indian Reserve property. I remember my Dad mentioning that the annual lease was $35. But we couldn't buy it. I have been told that the private dwellings are all gone, now. At the time that I was going to university, there was a push to get the native Indians into university. These are the people that I met up there, the First Nations people, but now they learned to be lawyers. And now they've got three-piece suits. "Okay, let's renegotiate."

I understand that they have now developed the waterfront property at Gibsons, and I'd love to go up there. One of those things. One of these days.

In the winters we used to ski up at Hollyburn. We were living in Kerrisdale. I would take the earliest morning streetcar down to Vancouver and wait for the first West Vancouver ferry over to Hollyburn. I would pack my skis – no buses running that early on a Sunday in West Vancouver – and walk up to Heywood to pick up my buddy and we'd go up and ski all day. If you had a hundred dollars worth of boots, ski poles, skis, wow! You were in the elite class.

No chair lift. There were a few rope tows available. I remember vividly my mother getting me a leather jacket. Not the black leather jackets the bikers have today. I wore it skiing and I got into a rope tow, which grabbed it and tore the front of the jacket. I caught hell for that.

"I just paid 28 dollars for that leather jacket!"

2. Norm Schmidt – First Years in Surrey

I started working as a cleanup boy at age 14 in an optical lab. This was a Saturday job. Gradually, they would say, "Come and see what we're doing here." Next it was, "Now you know that job, let's try you on this one."

First thing I know, I'm the utility boy for my summer holidays. I couldn't work as quickly as the other guys, but I knew the whole thing.

After I graduated from UBC I was working as a salaried practitioner optometrist in Vancouver and decided I don't like the big city. Even though I was a Vancouver boy, I wanted to get out. An old practice was for sale in New Westminster, so I bought it. But being young and aggressive, I was looking for extra work, and somehow I got phoned one day by Oakalla Prison farm. "We're looking for an optometrist to come in and do eye exams here. Would you be interested?"

I said, "Let me get back to you."

I was deeply in debt. I've lived with debt all my life. So I took on going into Oakalla, and I thought, "If I do this for two years, doing eye exams in there once a month, I'll pay off some of my indebtedness." 25 years later they shut the place down on me.

I met a lot of very interesting people. Men and women. Even up to the former Minister of Forestry. He was awaiting trial for selling forest licenses under the table. Later he was convicted, and he ended up doing Federal time, and they sent him out to one of the nicer jails up the Valley where they taught him to be a piano tuner. There's a message there somewhere; I don't know what it is.

This old practice that I purchased in New West was from an old-timer and he manufactured his own glasses, assembled them. This was something I had earned my way through university with. I had the grinder in my office, and I could grind the lenses right there.

This would be in the 40s, 50s. People were wearing frames that were gold filled. I learned silver and gold soldering. You don't do that anymore.

We got married in 1955 and we decided I wanted to be closer to my work out here in Surrey. I remember when I told my mother that we had bought a house out here in Riverside she almost burst into tears because she was living in Kerrisdale, and we would never meet. My Dad was a High School teacher, and of course the next year he took early retirement and where did they go? To Arizona for six months of the year.

Moving out to Surrey was quite an experience. Riverside shopping area had just opened up and I remember 108th Avenue was unpaved at that time. Way out at the end of civilization.

I had met this chiropractor who had just built a clinic down on Grosvenor Road in Whaley. Just making conversation over a glass of wine, I said, "You wouldn't happen to have a space there for an optometrist, would you?"

He said, "Yes, I do."

So I started going out to Whaley on Thursday afternoons, and his receptionist would make appointments for me, but suddenly I found that I was full up. I had to come out Tuesday mornings as well. Within a short time, let's say a year and a half or so, I said, "Forget about New West. I'm out here full time."

Everything happened so quickly I just said, "I'll card the people and say, 'Hey, I'm just across the river'." But people don't just cross the river, especially on the Patullo Bridge. But it was onward and upward from then on.

We married in 1955, and had 4 kids in 4 years. Then we finally found out what was causing it.

My wife had a sister that was 8 years older than her. I had a brother that was 7 years younger. Even before we got married, we said, "You know, if a family comes along, we want the kids to be close together so they are socializing together." And it worked out that way.

Property out here was cheap in those days. $12,000 bought us a brand new house in Birdland in behind Riverside. Hamilton Harvey was eventually the shopping centre, and then the Dell shopping centre.

We sold Birdland in 1962 and went to Bolivar Heights. It was funny. We decided it would be appropriate, maybe we should think of a larger house. Even though this house was brand new with a full basement. We had plans of finishing the basement, either as a game room or extra bedrooms, but one day I went down with a pencil and paper and said, "The sewer goes out three feet off the floor."

The area had been built for no-basement homes. So we couldn't expand. So I was having lunch with a real estate agent named Ian MacNaughton, and he said, "I have a house that I cannot sell. It's overbuilt for the area. It's on a double lot, an executive home, if you can use that word. Three bathrooms."

Ideal. Later on I put in a fourth. With teenagers an extra bathroom is a necessity.

Ian suggested we go look at this big house. "There's things in it you'll enjoy."

I remember we had a key to the back door, and we came in, and there was a mud room, washer-dryer place, then we came into the kitchen, and I vividly remember my wife saying, "Oh, Norm! Oh Norm."

A huge kitchen with a dishwasher. Unheard of in 1962.

The asking price was $50,000 – a double lot. Ian said, "I've had no offer at that price."

Foolishly, I said, "Tell him I'm offering him $22,000."

I didn't realize I was talking to a professional, and he has to take that offer to the owner.

We didn't hear from this guy. He was in financial trouble in California. We didn't hear from him for almost a month.

I said, "Oh, we've insulted him."

Finally he made contact and said, "I won't come down to $22 thousand but I'll come down to $23."

Now, they've called my bluff. This is a poker game, and my bluff has been called. Where am I going to get the money?"

Now, my wife, by this time, is in love with this dishwasher, and so she said, (In fact, I think this was one of those pillow talk things in the middle of the night,) she said, "Honey, I know how we can buy the house. I'll go back to work."

So we bought the house.

She was a nurse. She hadn't worked all these years.

We had decided; we had a two-year plan, that she would work for two years. She went to St. Mary's Hostpital in New Westminster, working nights.

My business was on Grosvenor, and I ended up over on 108th. I would drop Karen, the youngest, off at kindergarten in the morning. I would pick her up and bring her home for lunch. Mum would get the other kids off to school and then have a nap. Then Karen would have a nap, so it all worked together.

You make it work, but we never saw each other. At least it solved one problem: no more kids.

She finally retired at 57.

Then in about 1973 or 74 I moved to a rental property. By that time my practice had grown. I didn't need a storefront high-visibility place. I had a following, and people would follow me wherever I went. So I rented this property across from the Lions Football Centre, it's a brick building. The Canadian Legion is across the way.

Finally after about five years, I said, "What am I paying rent for? I can buy this."

The property was owned by a physician, and at Christmas time the rental agreement had come up, and I remember going to his home and saying, "Well, look, I'll sign for another year's lease," and as I left, wishing him and his wife best of the season, I said to him something to the effect. "Unless you want to sell me the building."

He said, "No, no, I don't want to sell the building. Oh, no."

Three weeks later I get a big letter delivered. He had offered me to purchase the building, giving me exactly one week to make up my mind. I didn't have the money! I owed the bank this much, but somehow it worked. I was still keeping my days out at Oakalla, and also out at the Haney Correctional Institution. It was fun for the kids at school, "Can you come and do such-and-such on Saturday?"

"No we can't because our Dad's in jail."

When I was working at Haney Correctional I used to have lunch there, and there was this chubby little social worker and we hit it off. We would have to be reminded. "Listen, you guys are here to work. Get in there and do your...whatever it is you do."

His name was David. David Barrett. He just passed away recently.

Anyway, I bought the building. I was able to rent half it out, and that meant I got free rent, and I kept it. I sold it when I retired.

That's when I got insight into capital gains. My accountant, said, "Oh, you've had a good year, Norm. You sold the office building."

And I said, "Yeah."

He said, "You've attracted capital gains. This isn't your home. You have to pay tax on it."

I wrote a big cheque. It's always been a sore point to me that I write the cheque to Income Tax and they take it to Ottawa and spend it on the other provinces.

My wife changed hospitals about 1970. She'd had surgery and then she came over to the hospital on 112th, Florence Nightingale Hospital, which was just around the corner from our house. It's common today, to work and live 20 miles apart. I could and did walk to work on occasion. We only had one car, so if my wife had something to do, "I'll get home from work somehow. Don't worry."

111A was a gravel road with open ditches. There were cows across the street from our house. We've come a long way.

3. Norm Schmidt – Working at Oakalla

The agreement was that I would do eye exams on 12 inmates on a Saturday afternoon. On occasion they would bring a couple of women down from the women's building. This was welfare-type work. Nothing exotic, just basic. Anyway one gal, a street lady, said, "I don't have any money here, but how about we make a deal, and I can come around to your office and we can conclude the payment there."

I didn't respond to that.

Looking back, these people who are doing time are no different from the rest of the population. I remember once I was working and an incident happened at another part of the facility, and they had a lockdown.

They closed the cage door, and when the "clink" happened the reality hit me. The place was in total shutdown, and I'm sitting with a couple of inmates, and we get to talking and I realize "I'm locked in here, and if something happens..." And, you know, nothing ever happened.

I was smoking in those days. Everybody smoked in those days. I was usually assigned one or two inmates to do my paperwork for me. Cigarettes are a currency and I'd make a point of leaving my pack on the desk. I'd say, "Help yourself."

One of them mentioned, "I notice you're generous with your cigarettes. You mind if we grab a couple?" Because that's money in the jail. "Matter fact, Doc, if you say the right words, something would be delivered to you on the street, inside a cigarette package.

You would bring it in and you'd throw the cigarettes down for us to help ourselves, and when you picked the cigarettes up, you'd find something inside. Hard cash."

I never did. I talked it over with my wife, though. I said, "They're talking $300 a trip. It wouldn't take long to cut the mortgage on the house down." But we thought about it for some length, and we decided, "No!" The drugs come in anyway, but I didn't have to be part of it.

And I never had any trouble with any of the inmates. I had a service that they needed. The police always break their glasses. I'd come in and their glasses would always be broken, and I'd have to replace them. A guy who can't read in jail with all this time on his hands…"

They were the dregs from society. Everything from bank robbers to the teenagers I met up in the Haney Correctional Institute.

That's where I had my friendship with Dave Barrett. Oddly enough, he was NDP. He ran in the Haney area, and one thing he was going to do, he was going to close the Haney Correctional down. "It's an abomination." He was a social worker and a good guy, and he hated it.

4. Norm Schmidt – My Mother's Pension

She would have been working as an operator for BC Tel at that time. When my Dad decided to take early retirement at age 60, she got in touch with the Chief Operator and said, "I'm giving my notice that I'm going to quit at the end of June, at the end of the school year. My husband is retiring, so I'm going to quit."

The Chief Operator – I can almost see this happening – "Don't say anything more. Let's have coffee together." So they went out for coffee, and he said, "I cannot tell you inside, but there is a pension fund coming."

General Telephone and Electronics owned BC Tel, and they were going to bring in a pension. Unfortunately it wasn't retroactive. But my mother did get a piddly little pension in American funds. And this was her pin money.

I have something that I'd love to share with you, here. When I settled her estate, I was dealing with General Telephone, and they gave me a nice letter, "Sorry about your mother passing, blah, blah, blah, but here's the final payout."

Nothing happened for three months. Then I get a letter from New York, saying, "Very sorry with respect to that last letter, we made a mistake in calculating the benefit. Please find enclosed the correct cheque." It was a cheque drawn on a bank in New York for ten cents. I still have that on my wall.

I didn't cash it, and they can't close that account down because this idiot in Canada won't cash that cheque. I've been able to tell that story so often! Big business gone crazy. How much did it cost them to have a cheque drawn, and somebody had to write it, sign it, pay for the stamp...

5. Norm Schmidt – Retirement

Something I brought into the family marriage. My parents had a weekend cottage at Lyndale Beach, Cultus Lake, and for some reason I had acquired a piece of property there. Cost me $250. I remember pillow talk with my wife one night, she saying something like, "You know, Norm we've got 4 kids. Maybe we should build our own place at Cultus Lake." Which ended up being our retirement home in later years.

I retired in 1982, and we were empty nesters for about 5 years. Then in '87 my wife was diagnosed with colon cancer, and had 7 years battling this cancer. That took a lot of time because the cancer clinic is in Vancouver. It was a long battle, planning the retirement and moving from the house on 111a and renovating the house at Cultus at the same time.

Don't ever take an old house and try to fix it up. This was an old house, and it was done with slave labour. Nothing was square. When we finished the inside with gyprock, the men cursed me at great length, because nothing fitted.

We moved up there in 1994, We saw all the kids get married and she did get to see our first grandson. We ended up with 4 grandsons. One's a firefighter now, and one is almost a firefighter.

We just got everything set up, and six months after moving up there, she passed away. You work so hard and retire, then die at sixty-four.

So I was living at Cultus lake, my vacation/retirement home. My wife had lost her battle with cancer in November, and one of my sons, Drew, came in one day in January and said, "Dad, what are you doing here?" It was pissing rain out. He said, "You've got an RV out there. Why aren't you down in California?"

By that time Karen had come up, and something that the surviving spouse has to deal with is handling the clothing.

Karen offered, "Do you want me to deal with Mum's clothing?"

I said, "Please do." Because I couldn't touch it.

So then Drew came up and said, "For God's sake, Dad, you've got an RV out there, get in it and go and get some sunshine."

I went to bed that night, thinking, "That's good advice. Get a change of scene." The personal stuff had been taken out of her closet, and I guess I'd started making some kind of adjustment, mentally.

The following morning I went out to make sure the fifth wheel travel trailer was ready to go, but there were her toothbrush and her slippers.

I said, "This isn't gonna work. I've gotta get rid of this vehicle. There's too many memories."

So we took it down to Langley, and I took it in and I said, "Cash me out."

"Well, wouldn't you like to have an RV of some kind? We've got an RV here that we're featuring."

It was a 32-foot class-A motor home. Total overkill for just me and my cat. Me and my cats, in time. I've travelled all over North America in this motor home. And it's the most expensive way to travel. You get about seven miles to the gallon. It's got disc brakes. It's a bus. So if you need a brake job, you can't just get one of those 58-dollar jobs. You need a real big one.

I always had it in mind that when you took it in for repairs, the guys would say, "Go and have coffee, we'll tell you when it's ready." With this beast I come back and they say, "We happened to have the front wheels off, and we noticed that your front end needed some work." So there's another $300 job. I've heard it so often. But that vehicle took me and my various cats all over, and that's something I've had fun with. Me and my cats.

Now, at the senior's centre where I'm residing, I say, "I've just come in here, but I'm not here alone. I've got my 19-year-old girlfriend with me." I've got a lot of mileage out of that. My cat's still with me.

So that's it. I've outlived almost everybody. I have to keep thinking, "Am I really 88?"

6. Norm Schmidt – Travelling With a Gun

About 1944, I'm in High School, and they have cadets. Somehow I got thrust into the rifle team. I was a good shot. Dominion Marksman was the thing, and you get a bronze, silver, and gold pin you can wear. I've gone hunting once. With my cousin. And suddenly I thought, "Oh! If I see that Bambi with the big brown eyes!" So I know about guns.

Even though I had a 32 foot motor home that somehow was worth $80,000, I'm a cheap son-of-a-gun and I'd stay out at the rest areas when I was travelling in the States. The family got kind of worried about Dad, travelling through the United States unarmed. So I went to a gun store in Texas, and I said, "I'm a Canadian citizen. Can I purchase a gun here?"

"Why, certainly, sir."

They did a background check on me. I purchased a revolver for $200. They did a search. They had to phone some clearing house in that county to see if my name was on a list. That was it. Then I'm travelling and I say, "Well, I'm armed and dangerous, now."

I'm coming back, and I'm looking forward to crossing that border and getting back into Canada, and suddenly I say, "Oh, my gosh, I've got a six-gun here. I can't just show up. They'll seize it."

So I took it to some place where I could check it, and they gave me a great big form the RCMP have, a permit to transport a restricted weapon. I had to take a course and prove my competency. But over the years I have acquired three handguns. People find out, "Norm is a gun nut." Typically the story I get, is "Grandpa died and we found this gun in his stuff. What do we do?"

I would tell them, "Take it to the police."

They don't like to carry it, they don't want to deal with the police "I gift it to you, Norm."

"Thanks a lot. Now I have to register it." Drew has all of these firearms, and I've got to get in touch with him. There's several hundred dollars worth of them.

Family Lore

Editor's Note: Dave Johnston lives in Langley Lodge, and we had two story-telling sessions there with him and several members of his family.

1. Janice Johnston – Introduction

Dave and I are both from Vancouver, born and raised. We went to different schools and we didn't meet till high school. Then we started dating, and got married from there.

We used the beaches. We were Jericho Beach people. We were always at the water till long after the season was over. They took everything all up and put it away for the winter, and here we were, still going down there.

We swam, and sometimes we had boats, sometimes the kids would take the boats out, then come back in and see us for a bit, then go out again.

Norm covered all of BC for a line of automotive equipment, and then started a power washer company called Hotsy Automotive, selling and maintaining steam cleaners and pressure washers. He went out of town upcountry, and sometimes I drove for him.

I was a stay-at-home mum with three kids. But I also would take Dave to work at times, because he'd get stuck. He was clinically blind from his fifties, and now is totally blind.

2. Dave Johnston – Logging on Vancouver Island.

I was 15 years old, and it was my first real job, in the summer of 1944. I reported to work on Vancouver Island. We took off on a Monday morning from Duncan to Lake Cowichan, right out to the west coast of Vancouver Island where they had the locomotive all set up. It was pulling the logs out of the bush. It was quite a hilly area, and you can imagine the loggers pulling the logs out on steep mountains. Anyhow I asked someone what he wanted me to do.

He said, "Take that strawline," The strawline is a long cable. They haul a log out and then take the chokers back with the strawline.

I said, "Where do you want it?"

He said, "Across that log over the river." The river was 50-60 feet across. The line was quite heavy. The boss said, "That's your initiation here." It must have been 50 or 60 pounds of cable on my shoulder and climbed up on this tree which was felled across the river. Across the river I went, balancing on the log.

So I did. I tell you, I was prepared to go for a swim. Everybody was waiting breathlessly to see me fall. But I made it across the river, inch by inch. So I got all the way to the other side, and I had to climb the mountain with the straw line on my back. It was noon when I finally arrived. I soon learned that loggers knew how to hide the path through the bush to go up and down the mountain. I got much better at it.

Anyhow, we were there one Saturday, and it was very early, because it was fire season in the bush, and they cut us off. The Fire Marshal came by and said, "You can't work with a locomotive, because sparks fly and there's going to be a forest fire."

Sure enough, we all got undressed and went down to go swimming in the pond under a tree, and all of a sudden the scream came from the tracks that there was a fire started. "Get the hell out of there quickly!"

We did. We got out of there, and we started highballing along the railroad tracks. There were a couple of fallers came out of the bush. I guess they'd absorbed all the heat off the rocks. It was a very hot day. They went berserk. The rest of the loggers jumped on these two, because they were going to go over the side of the bank into the steep part of the mountain, trying to get away from the fire.

It really shook me up.

I worked 24 hours that day, and every day for a month I fought forest fire 12 hours a day. For a kid going to school, 15 years old, it was a big deal.

So I came back to school and I was relaying all my stories to the kids in my classes. The next year I was going to go back, but I got interested in mining, so I went to the Silbak Premier mine up on the Alaskan Panhandle. That was an education, because it was really in the wilds. We got there by boat. We had to go by Union Steamship. They put me down in the hold. It was a two-day trip at that time. So I woke up in the middle of the night. There was rustling around. There were a couple of Indian girls bedding down next to me. I grabbed my wallet and put it in my shoe.

I finally got to Silbak Premier. I didn't really care for that place. It was too much in the wild. I had a job driving the little ore carts.

The next year, rather than going to Silbak Premier, I went to Braelorn. I'll tell you, that was a real education. That's one of the richest gold mines in the world. In the morning when I arrived at the station downtown to get picked up the limousine service that took us to Braelorne had to pick up a man that was let out of the jail in Burnaby. He sat between me and another guy and he chattered all the way till we got to Braelorne, which was about 4 in the afternoon. Once we settled into the bunk house, he says to me, "Come on, I'll buy you dinner."

So we went into the restaurant and sat down and the cook and waiter were a couple of French Canadians. They were talking and laughing and carrying on, and all of a sudden the door opened and in came this big, huge guy. He must have been 6'6" or 6'7."He was an Indian. Pete Swaine was his name. He wanted to be everybody's friend. He'd been drinking all afternoon. He put his arms around us. We were sitting on the stools in the café.

He wanted to buy us a drink.

This little gangster friend that I'd picked up told him to go and play with his bow and arrows or he'd kick his ass out the door. The guy picked up a chair and broke it over the counter of the restaurant. That was my first encounter with what was going on in the mine.

Every Saturday night everybody got drunk out of their minds and got into a fight. We used to go up to the dance hall and watch the activities because there was always a fight over Pete Swaine's daughters, who were good-looking girls. We were stir-crazy back then.

3. Dave Johnston – Working at Braelorn Mines

I went to Sylvan Premier up in the Alaskan Panhandle by myself. I was about 16 years old. Uncle Hal helped me to get there. I did that, and the next year I went to Braelorn, which was one of the richest gold mines in the world. So I went there and I came back to school and I was telling all the stories about the miners and what kind of characters they were.

So the next year there were 30 guys from McGee High School went to Braelorn Mines. Two of them became big alcoholics, and they all learned to gamble.

Braelorn was a gold mine. You drilled into the rock at a level rate until you came to a station, and then they sank a shaft that was around 1200 or 2000 feet or whatever it was so I got used to working underground in the dark. You'd think that blindness would bother me, but it was nothing like working in the dark.

I started out on a mucking machine, and then I graduated from there to being a helper in a shaft where the miner was a European miner from Latvia. I was his helper, and he was a highball performer. At first he didn't like me at all; I got in the way, but he soon found out that I could work as fast as he could and probably better, and work we did.

After two weeks he said to me, "Come on, kid, I'm going to buy you a beer."

So we went to the bar, and who should be in there but a prostitute he dealt with. That's all I'll say about that.

No, I didn't go anywhere near that angle. I was 16 at the time.

Anyway, he was a character, and he got into a very serious accident somewhere, and he followed me all the way to UBC. I went to UBC for a couple of years. In order for him to get some financial help after his accident, he could work, but he needed help.

I went to UBC but I didn't finish. I quit because I wasn't inclined to be a student. I was taking First Year Arts. I just knew it wasn't for me. Anyhow, I did poorly, If I had to do it over again, I guess I'd persevere and get my education, but I didn't think it was necessary at the time.

I didn't mind working and I could find work for myself.

4. Dave Johnston – Ethnic Differences in the Mine

When I first went to Braelorne we got on the elevator to go down the shaft to the level we worked at, ten hundred feet down, and I noticed there were a bunch of French Canadians and a bunch of Newfoundlanders, and they were always hassling each other. Open brawls on Saturday night. Anyhow they all came in and they were arguing on the way in, and the Frenchmen put their lunch pails on the bench, to come back and eat them later. One of the Newfies drove nails into the lunch boxes and put a stick of powder in there and blew the lunch box all over the station. That's the kind of antics that went on in that place.

In Braelorne they have an elevator shaft. Four people could ride the shaft down to the level you worked at. Anyhow, the power kicked off. What happens when the power kicks off on those elevators, they freefall. There's one single wire rope holding the thing. It bottomed out and the cage started to bounce. We all ended up on our noses. We got up and put our helments with our lamps back on. It scared the hell out of me. I thought I'd bought my ticket.

5. Dave Johnston – Career

After I finished working in Braelorn I decided I didn't want to be a miner, stuck out in the middle of nowhere. So I got a job with Taylor, Pearson and Carson. It was an automotive parts house in Vancouver. That was a good training ground for the future.

I met a guy there that I'd known in Braelorne. He was heading off to South America to work in a mine down there. He wanted me to go with him. I darned near went, but somewhere along the line I met Jan, and I decided life with her was more interesting than working in the bush. So I skipped that. He went down and did well. He looked me up when he came back.

In Grade 4 in school I found out that my eyes were bad. They put me in a class where I had to wear glasses all the time. I was pretty good at sports, so it was a wonder I didn't scratch my glasses. I tolerated my eye condition all the way through school until I got working with Taylor, Pearson. It turned out that I finally got a job as a salesman, somewhere in the 60s.

We had three kids, and they're the best things in my life. Hal, Judi, and Charles. You have to be lucky to have three wonderful kids like that.

I got married and I was able to advance my education business-wise by being hired by Black and Decker to be their BC rep. I did that for a while, and the opportunity arrived – you always take advantage of opportunities when they present themselves – to get into business for myself with a couple of automotive product lines. I took advantage of that. Big mistake. I went broke. But that's part of learning.

May 18th I'll be 89. My mother lived till 91. Her Dad, my grandfather, he was 88. So I think if things go okay, if these girls in this place (Langley Lodge) don't get mad at me.

6. Dave Johnston – The Cabin

My Uncle George had a cabin at buccaneer Bay on Thormanby Island, just out of Secheldt. It was my Dad and two brothers who originally started going there. He eventually sold it to rich doctors.

We went up there with our kids and still enjoyed going after it was sold. We then went to Vaucroft, just up the island, and up to Savory and places like that. The kids still go in their boats.

7. Dave Johnston – The Accident

My Dad's Uncle Hal and a couple of buddies went up to the cabin to reminisce about their youth for the weekend. Of course, they drank a lot on the way. The Scotch whiskey was flowing. They never stopped pouring. They tied the boat up to the wharf and loaded all their stuff in.

They got out in the water, and I guess somebody made the wrong move, and the boat capsized. Hal was a great swimmer: top-notch. They would never think of putting life jackets on. That was in October some time, and the water chills up; you can't stay in more than five minutes or you're dead. Hal kept moving because he was an alcoholic and his blood was pretty thin so the cold water didn't really affect him. When he reached the wharf outside the cabin, he got out of the water and collapsed. When he woke up in the morning he staggered up to the cabin and looked out. The tide was low, and there were the two bodies lying on the beach.

Uncle Hal would never go up to Buccaneer Bay again after that.

Hal lived in Honduras then, and he would come back to Vancouver to look people up. He graduated cum laude as a mining engineer. He certainly had people he had to see down in town.

Our son is also in mining, and that was kind of interesting. We'd have parties or gatherings, and Dave's mother was the instigator of all of it. She'd put the party on, and he'd supply the grub. It was quite colourful. He was always the hero. He came with stories. He was a man of mystery.

My grandmother always thought he was in the CIA because he was always having these secret meetings. We were there when a group of people that he knew from Honduras came to Vancouver and came to a party. It wasn't a big party, just a few.

These two fellows started talking about, "remember those guys…" It was Che Guevara they were talking about.

And that was the end. He knew them and everything, but he tried to squelch that talk. He didn't want the family knowing. We didn't want to know, either.

He always seemed to live somewhere, and then there was this unrest and he was moved to somewhere else. He lived in Panama, and he lived in Brazil, and 18 years in Africa, and then he moved to South Africa, but then he came to work as the #2IC on the Harmac plant over in Nanaimo. The head engineer there was a British military engineer so he hired Uncle Hal to be his 2IC building the Harmac plant.

8. Dave Johnston – The Boat in the Back Yard

I always wanted a boat for the Lower Mainland and up the Sunshine Coast. Places like Pender Harbour, where I grew up at Buccaneer Bay. Every summer we went to Buccaneer Bay. So I always wanted a big boat so I could go over to Half-Moon Bay or Pender Harbour or whatever.

It was 21 feet. I bought the ribs for it and went from there. But I changed the chassis to a more modern, up-to-date version from what it was. It was really designed to be a speedboat, but I made it into a cabin cruiser. It was made of plywood with fiberglass over.

And all the neighborhood kids played in the boat while I was building it. I think I had more water in it than around it. One of the neighbours had his eye on it. I decided I was going to get rid of it, sell it, because it was just going too slow. I wasn't a natural-born carpenter. I didn't have the skills to fabricate this thing properly.

So anyhow he came one day and said, "Hi," and said, "If you ever want to sell it let me know."

I said, "You just happen to be talking to the right guy."

So I sold it to neighbors from across the street,

He finished it and got it in the water. One day he was coming across from Horseshoe Bay to Jericho, and he started to slow down, and he couldn't figure out why he was slowing down. Well, the sheets of plywood didn't adhere properly, and they peeled off and the boat filled with water. He just made it to Spanish Banks, where he ran it aground before it sank. For years, we'd be out on another boat and we'd see the old boat, and the kids would say, "Oh, Dad, there's our boat. Don't tell anybody that was our boat."

Johnston – The Family.

parents included us in everything, from the boating, sports, life, to having friends, dinners. They demonstrated a caringness for each other and all of us that was beyond belief. We grew up in a very loving home with a wonderful experience living in the heart of Kerrisdale and going to good schools. If there was a dream to grow up, I'm sure we had it. The parents were the truth. They loved each other, they dedicated their lives to each other, and the kids came through with no chance of failing.

10. Hal Johnston – Boating stories.

We were very keen fishermen and entered the Sun Free Salmon Derby on occasion and had a great time fishing around Horseshoe bay, coming across other fishermen's lines and getting tangled. I learned a vocabulary that I was not quite sure of as a young man, but hanging around my father and hanging around my mother's father, Eddy Lewis, otherwise known as "Pappy," there was never a loss for expletives.

I enjoyed a very fortunate education from two men that I admired the most in my life. When I took to boating Dad had bought a boat after the one he built in the back yard. He fixed up a second one, a 14-foot Sangstercraft, and put a 40-horse Johnson on the back of that. Then he traded up to a 19-foot Grew.

We would go out on Saturdays. This boat had a habit of conking out, so my principal job was to stand on the front of the boat and take my jacket off and wave to any boats passing by that might be able to tow us back to the dock. We just could not understand how it was so easy to get this thing started and get out there, but it always died on the way back. We always had stories and events, and my Mum always brought sandwiches, and maybe my grandmother or somebody along.

Young Charles and Judi of course got worked into this culture of boating, and it all continued right from the moment we left the house with the boat on the trailer to the moment we launched it at the Burrard Civic Marina, and the joy that the family experienced watching other boaters have the same trouble that we had, launching their boats and knocking their motors off and dropping their lunches overboard, yelling and screaming at one another; it was an endless source of joy. We started taking our dinners down to the boat dock to watch the folly. It was total entertainment.

So I naturally got into boating, and stuck close to the boating crowd, and I found out that the salty dog types were my kind of people. Without any real training in boating I took to the water with a great deal of desire, but often ran into the same problems that my father experienced. No training, no practical safety training, very little mechanical ability, and always the baptism by fire at sea.

So I would come back and tell my stories to my friends, and after a while my stories were equally notorious, and they took up a collection and decided that I would be the nominee for taking the Power Squadron course and getting certified, because nobody could have so many boating incidents as I had. I came across it naturally: my father.

When they got married my Mum and Dad were up at Bucaneer Bay. One of the great stories was that Dad ran out of cigarettes and jumped in the boat with my mother and got halfway across. The boat conked out. While he monkey-wrenched the motor, he had my mother rowing the rest of the way across Welcome Pass, which is a dangerous body of water at the best of times.

Having heard all that and having lived it, and then having a correct course myself, I bought a bigger boat. I talked Dad into selling the 19-footer and going in with me on a 24-foot Grew. That expired at one point in life and I went on to buy a 34-foot Uniflite. It had 3208 Caterpillar turbo diesels in it. It was a rocket boat. It was the one that I always wanted, and being the fisherman and now certified as a safe boater, I thought it would be a good idea to give it to my Dad, and he could go out and experience what I was enjoying.

Jerry Dress was a part of this equation. I would be comfortable with my father and Jerry going off in my boat, because Jerry was mechanically inclined, and my Dad knew boating. So I thought the two of them would have no trouble. But of course mutiny is soon to follow at sea when one won't follow the other. I guess these two guys went off with their wives and decided to conquer the coast. In this boat they could get just about anywhere.

How they got into Aaron Rapids at the tide change is beyond me. But I got stories from my mother that the refrigerator dislodged itself and emptied onto the floor, and that the boat was rocking from side to side in the most treacherous conditions.

Now I've gone up there and done Aaron Rapids myself, and I would not recommend it to anybody. Knowing these guys at this point took my boat to that extreme on the first pass just tells me that it's never going to be any different for my grandchildren, whom I'm looking forward to training. But I'm going to start them with the boating course, safe boating.

We could always swim, because our parents were great swimmers, but when you're in these boating situations you really don't have a second chance. Your first mistake could be your last.

So there was joy and adventure, and eventually discipline, and the boating continues today on my side, and now goes on to our kids. I can't wait to get Judi's kids and Tom's kids, and anybody who wants to be a part of it. It's a culture; we learned it. My parents brought it forward and included us in it.

So we have aspirations on bigger boats, now. We're going to do it somehow or other. If I can give you one comment that my Dad gave me and that always stuck true in the back of my mind. When his father and the three brothers sold Buccaneer Bay I was ten years old; Judi would have been eight. Dad was heartbroken. It wasn't a place we could afford to buy at that point. The brothers had something in mind, and I think they sold Buccaneer Bay for $3,500 and took trips to Europe or wherever they went, and my Dad said to me at that point, I remember it clear as day, he said, "We're boaters now. We're going to take our waterfront with us."

That's been the attitude we've had ever since. We've never looked for another piece of property; we've always looked for a bigger boat

11. Hal Johnston – *Dad on a Bicycle*

What was fun was that we would hear stories. Dad had bad eyes, but Jerry would get him out on his bike, and Dad would be following Jerry all over the place, whether it was down in California or up here going around Stanley Park. And we obviously feared for our father's life when he went out there, because he wasn't seeing what Jerry was seeing, and Jerry didn't really give a hoot about that.

Many years later my mother would take Dad out on the bike. I knew he was in traffic, and I knew he couldn't see her. She would ring the bell so he could hear it and follow her.

I've seen the result of this B-Train activity. I saw them cutting across in front of my truck when I was driving at the corner of Blanca and 16th Avenue on the edge of the Endowment Lands. I saw my mother take off the road onto a dirt path, ringing the bell, and I saw my father follow onto the dirt path blind as a bat and roll his bike. I screamed in my car, "What are you doing?"

I knew he was just trying to keep up, but I got out and I ran over and picked my Dad up and dusted all the leaves off and I said, "What are you doing?"

"He said, 'Following your Mother.'"

I said, "How is this working for you?"

It was amazing that through his handicap and his love for her and the outdoor activities. These were very outgoing, active people. From tennis to extreme boating to their friends and many social events. That's about the most normal life I've seen two people live, and I'm sure happy to be part of it.

I mean, the characters that would show up at our door and tell their stories. It was never-ending. Politics got into it. We had tremendous discussions, family discussions where everybody got a chance to talk. You became somewhat opinionated, you liked what you heard in certain respects, you learned to respect the other opinion. It was a very vital time to grow up in a neighbourhood with really cool people, and just the respect for our parents and that's the same respect we hold for each other today, because they lived the life. They lived the dream.

The Perfect Storm

Sometimes something unique happens to us, simply because a bunch of normal things happened to get together at exactly the right time to create something far from normal. It can be the right place at the right time or the wrong place at the wrong time. Then we have the most wonderful, the most awful, or the just plain unexplained. The perfect storm.

1. *Gordon Long – A Perfect Storm of Feathers*

This story began on a perfectly normal day, during a perfectly normal activity. But I was in the right place at the right time, and the wind was blowing the right amount in the right direction, and for two minutes my life side-stepped into the fantastical. And then the moment was over, and life went back to normal.

Now, in order to understand how normal this situation was, it helps to know two things about the flight of birds. First, birds always fly forwards. Only hummingbirds can fly backwards. However, if there is a wind blowing in the opposite direction and the bird flies exactly the speed of the wind, then almost any bird can hover. Raptors and gulls do it all the time. So it is theoretically possible for a bird that is sitting on the ground, if he really likes that spot on the ground, to fly up against the wind and hover, perhaps while a threat goes away, and then settle back down on the exact same spot.

Theoretically possible.

And the second fact is about birds that fly closely bunched in flocks. Those birds all stay exactly the same distance from each other. It's coded into their genes. So if one bird moves a bit to the left, the whole flock shifts left exactly the same amount. Always the same distance apart.

Which brings me to my story.

My dog, Josh, is a Nova Scotia Duck Tolling Retriever, and he needs a lot of exercise, so we run every day. One late fall day a couple of years ago we were running on the dyke in Richmond, B. C. The dike in Richmond is a great place to run: smooth and level, with a lot of friendly people walking on it. But this particular day had started out with a huge rainstorm, and even at ten in the morning there was absolutely no one on the path.

So Josh and I were running merrily along, enjoying a strong, cool breeze and the sunshine breaking through the clouds, when we came around a corner.

And there, right in our way, was a huge flock of snow geese. This flock winters over in the slough between the dike and the North Arm of the Fraser River, a couple of thousand of them, so they're a common sight. In this case, there was a little field between the dyke and the slough, and they covered it completely, some of them spilling out onto the path on top of the dyke.

So, what am I going to do? I don't want to scare them away. But these are pretty tame geese. I have spent a lot of time training Josh not to chase ducks, so he's pretty cool with birds. I decide I'll slow down to a walk and just go straight on by, and see what they will do.

Well, they don't do much. As we walk past, the ones nearby waddle away, chatting with their friends the whole time. When we have gone by, they waddle back to the place they were standing. I look back, and there they are, evenly spaced across the field, with no evidence we have disturbed the flock at all. Those geese are tamer than I thought.

So Josh and I pick up the pace and run off down the dyke for a couple of kilometres, then turn around and run back.

When we get to the flock, they've moved inland. They now cover the top of the dyke completely for about fifty metres along the path. What am I going to do?

This seems a pretty good chance for an experiment. Josh is having no problem, bopping along beside me. I decide to slow down and walk exactly as I had before and see what they do. So I pull Josh in on a tight "heel" and pace forward.

Well, the geese don't waddle away. As we approach, those nearest to us begin to fly up in the air. And I think, "That's too bad, I didn't want to scare them away."

But did I mention the wind? There's a strong breeze blowing in our faces, and when the geese fly up, they don't go anywhere. They just rise straight into the air and hover on the wind. The ones nearest to us rise about five metres, but the ones farther away don't rise so far, and the geese about five meters to either side don't move at all. There in front of me is an arch of geese.

So we keep walking. And as we walk, more and more geese in front of us rise up, and soon we're walking in a tunnel of geese, all flying, all holding their position with the geese close to them, but only a few metres above the ground. So we walk farther down the tunnel, and I glance back. The geese we have passed under are sinking back to the ground, exactly where they rose from.

So now we're walking in a perfect dome of snow geese, with every bird the same distance from every other bird, and all of them about five metres from us.

Now, I had my phone with me, and I thought about trying to shoot some video. But I knew what would happen. Whatever we were doing was a precise element in this whole perfect scenario. As long as we moved exactly as we were, we sent exactly the right message to the geese to cause this behaviour. If I stopped, fiddled with my camera, maybe dropped the leash, I knew I would spoil this perfect moment. The geese would break formation and all I'd get would be a shot of a bunch of goose butts flying away. A dime-a-dozen picture.

So we just kept walking. And our perfect dome of big, white geese moved through the flock with us. When we got to the far side there were no more birds, and we walked out of the arch and into the sunshine. After a moment I turned to look back, and the birds were all back on the ground, still spaced out perfectly, as if we had never been there.

So Josh and I started running again. We went back to the car and drove home and finished off a perfectly normal day. I have no picture of this wonderful event, but I have treasured it up in my heart, and I will remember it forever. And now I am sharing it with you.

2. Marilyn Gerald's Weird and Wonderful

When we returned from Hawaii to Vancouver my daughter Christine was away at boarding school in Victoria. She was 14 years old. I got a phone call from Edmonton on a Tuesday night. It was that her grandfather had died. Her Greek grandfather on her father's side. Papoo we called him. I got a phone call that he had died.

The next morning, Wednesday. I got a call from Christine, saying "I had the worst nightmare that Papoo had died. "

I said, "Oh, dear. That's very strange. Well, you're going to be home on the weekend and we'll talk about it."

So she came home on the weekend and I told her that he had died that Tuesday night.

I thought that was fairly weird. Not so wonderful, but fairly weird.

And I guess Christine passed on some traits, because we were having Christmas with the Van Deusens at my father's apartment in Vancouver. Her son, Bryce, was 4 years old at the time. When they left, my daughter called me from the speaker downstairs. "Can you come and talk to Bryce?"

I said, "Sure, I'll come down."

I went down, and I'm talking to him, and he said, "I don't want Grandpa to die."

I said, "Well, Grandpa's a pretty old man." He was about 96 years old.

He said, "I don't want him to die."

I said, "He's going to die some time, Bryce, but let's not worry about that. It's Christmas, you know, and ...blah, blah, blah."

My father died that night.

3. Michael Barregor: Dad's Air Force Career

I don't know how much we can put into the book, but back in the 80s Mum and Dad took a holiday in Eurpoe and rented "The Orange Ox," a little Volkswagen hippy bus. They were driving outside of Frankfort, where we had lived, but about 60 miles out of town, Dad said, "Here's a good spot for us to have a picnic," and he pulled over. And it was just a concrete foundation

Mum laid out a blanket, and they were having a picnic lunch, and he said, "Do you remember all those years that you thought I was working in an office at the Air Force base? I was right here, six stories down, through three concrete, six-foot-deep walls with steel doors. That was where my office was."

And that's all we were allowed to know about his job.

It was the same when he worked in Metz. There is a beautiful Chateau du Mercie. Mum thought Dad was working in it. No, again on a trip, you know where the Maginot Line was? Outside of Metz. More bunkers with steels doors. That's where he worked.

And she thought he was working on the air base.

4. **Eve Baldwin– My Amah**

My Amah I had as a child in India. She mothered and smothered me. I was with her from about the age of two, I suppose, until I was about 10. She used to take me backwards and forwards from home to school and wait for me all day.

When I got to in India with the Air Force, believe it or believe it not, there was my amah waiting for me when I got off the boat. How she knew I was going to be there I will never know, but she was there to meet me. We were allowed one amah between three or four of us. But my amah wouldn't have any of that. She stayed by me, so I had to get special permission to have my own amah.

She came to Singapore with me. She wouldn't leave me. She was with me in Singapore the whole time. Then, two days before I left, she just lay down and died. She must have been coming up seventy something. Just two days. She knew that I was leaving, and two days before, she died.

I was on a cruise a few years ago with my friend, Red. We were lying around on deck chairs and my friend was talking to the woman next to her, and they were talking about children and school and things like that.

Red asked her, "Well, where did you go to school?'

"Oh," she said, "you wouldn't know my school. I went to a little school in Jagapoor in India."

"Hey," she jabbed me. "This woman went to the same school as you did."

I said, "Never. There was only one other English girl there."

She said, "That was me."

I said, "I don't believe it. She was an older girl."

She said, "You were the little girl with all the matted hair. I remember you and your amah who wouldn't let you out of her sight. She stood there and watched you all through school."

That was the same amah, all the way through my life. She was like a mother to me, you know.

5. **Karen MacGregor – Hair Salon Holdup**

My guests that came up from Houston, and the young 'uns asked how I felt about guns. I said, "If I see guns here, driving up country, it never bothers me, because what comes to my mind is they're for hunting." In their way of thinking a gun is to shoot somebody. That's their take on it versus mine. But I had an experience with guns here in Surrey in 1983.

I was working in a little hair salon, a corner shop. It was the early nineties. These guys on the street would sell products out of duffle bags. They'd be selling stuffed animals or whatever, cheap.

I was cutting this little girl's hair when these two guys came into the salon and pulled this thing out of a bag. They struggled to get it out of the bag: a couple of buffoons. They were saying to the people in the front, "Get on the floor! Get on the floor!"

And they looked at me, and I just continued cutting, and they said, "Get on the floor! Didn't you hear us? Get on the floor."

And that's when I realized it was a real gun. So I got the little girl down, and we just lay on the floor.

They were trying to open up a computer. It wasn't a till, it was a computer. But they kept pushing the buttons. "Open the till. Open the till!"

I kept saying, "It's not a till. The money's in a Tupperware under the counter."

It took them – you know, it might have only happened in a matter of three minutes, which felt like fifteen or twenty at the time– and then they grabbed my bag as well and they walked out.

There was an elementary school across the street that had just let out, and it was surreal, because everything just continued as a normal day, and we had just been held up.

We contacted the police, of course, trying to push 911 with hands just shaking completely. I went with the little girl and her parents. By fluke they were visiting from Prince George, and they were staying with an uncle just up the road from me. So we went in together and tried to do a character description, but to this day I don't think they've ever been found. At least I never heard anything.

It shakes a person up.

6. Eve Baldwin – Voodoo in Nigeria

This was in a place called Lokoja. My husband, Bob, worked in the radar station he had erected, training the Nigerian people there. John was a very nice young man, and he had recently got married. I think he was Ebo. A good worker.

Then one day he didn't come to work. Bob thought, "Well, okay, he's probably not feeling too good ."

He didn't turn up the next day, but his wife did. His young wife came up and she said, "Mister Bob, you come quick. You come quick see John."

So my husband said, "What's the matter with him?"

"He put big juju on him."

So Bob went and saw John. He was lying there. He was a black man, but he was turned a sickly grey. I went with my husband; I happened to be at the office and I went there with him. I have never seen a man that sickly grey.

What had happened, John had married Mary, but when she was a baby she had been sold by her parents to marry this older man. He found out that she had married John. He went to the juju man and put lots of money down to have him kill John to get Mary back for himself.

My husband thought, "Well, this isn't a case for medication." So he said to John, "How much did this man give the voodoo man."

John said it was about 20 English pounds.

So Bob took 40 pounds and went to see the juju man. I went with him. I wasn't going to miss this.

This juju man was just an ordinary-looking man. He just wore this beautiful embroidered gown and this hat. We met him in his house. Just an ordinary house. No stuff hanging around, nothing else. All I saw was this beautiful earthenware bowl that he kept fingering. He just put his hand on it and fingered it. When Bob put down 40 pounds, the juju man took the money, played around in the bowl, raised his arms like "It is done."

My husband and I looked at each other, and went away. "Did this work?"

It was getting late at night and we couldn't go back to tell John. Bob was called out during the night, so he was still at the radar station in the morning. John came back to work, as black as you wouldn't believe. Just like that.

I've never had anything to do with juju, I've never actually believed in it, but that I did see with my own eyes.

7. Josie McGinnis – Taking on the Government

My name is Josie McGinnis. I live in Delta, B. C. and I took on the government.

My husband died the 17th of November 1990, 39 days short of being 55 years old. I got a letter the beginning of January stating that I would not get his pension because he was not 55 years of age. That was a clause in it because it was registered under Quebec legislation. So I sat on it for a couple of weeks and then I took it to a referral lawyer first, and he told me, "Not interested, you'll never win."

So I said, "Thank you for your time. Here's my 85 dollars."

I decided to take it to the faculty of Law and let the students study it. They picked everything out, and I got a lovely lady by the name of Delaine Sardison, who took it on. She told me to go to Legal Aid.

They accepted me in Legal Aid because I was under a certain amount of income per year.

The company my husband worked for, they're all over the United States. I can't give you their name. I proceeded to send them letters and tell them that we were taking on this thing and wanted this changed. So we did.

I got some threatening letters from the head office, saying that I would never win, and don't bother carrying on. So we wrote back saying that we don't have to take this harassment. We'll take you on for harassment too, if you want.

And then I waited for the lawyer, and she did it all.

I wanted the pension money given to me and the pension law changed because that wasn't fair to anyone whose husband died before that age. Even 39 days short.

So my first lawsuit was asking the company to give me the pension. It was due to go to court four years later in April, and they settled in December.

The second lawsuit, we sent letters to the pension legislation office in Victoria, wanting this legislation changed because of discrimination. I went to the MLA in Delta at the time, I don't know who he was, and he said, "I'm not interested, I'm not even going to talk to you."

So I left, but I just kept plugging away. We went through the human rights department in Vancouver on Robson Street.

I didn't get any letters from the government until I won, and then the Worker's Compensation Board phoned me and wanted me to come to work for them.

We got a decision on the basis of discrimination because of age. So the government had to make the changes in the legislation.

Companies all have to pull their registered pensions out of Quebec and register them in B. C., because we have a pension registration here in Victoria. Now you can't register a pension for BC people in Quebec. And now below the age of 55 the survivor gets a pension on a sliding scale.

There was a lady in Richmond whose husband died at 46, and she was doing the same thing, and she got a settlement. There was a woman in St. Catharine's Ontario and she also got a settlement. I think they were going through it at the same time as I was, because they all came down at the same time.

It was a piece of legislation whose time had come.

My advice for people is to stand up for your rights. Go to Human Rights in Vancouver. They're very knowledgable. And the Faculty of Law at UBC.

8. Leo Ramirez – Car Bomb

I was a war correspondent and News Director for several radio stations in El Salvador during the 80s. I covered the civil war from 1982 to 1989.

That happened after I had been in Canada for three months. We were driving with a couple of other Latin American broadcasters from Toronto to Brampton on Highway 427. It was snowing, and about 5 o'clock in the evening.

We were mid way and I saw a white car on the side of the road with the emergency lights flashing. In El Salvador if you see a car like that you automatically think that it is a car bomb. So I said to the driver, Manuel from Dominican Republic, "Speed up. There is a car bomb."

He said to me with a little smile. "Leo, that is not a car bomb. That is a car that has mechanical trouble and it is on the side of the road. Leo, this is Canada. You are not in El Salvadore. You are not in a civil war any more. Please react that way."

I said, "Okay, well, I don't care. Speed up. To me, that is a car bomb."

So he sped up and we left that area and went to Ciaou Radio 730 in Brampton, a multicultural station where we had a radio show. Right now I have a radio show at UBC: Radio CITR 101.9 FM. I'm still alive, and having fun here in Canada.

9. Marilyn Gerald – Adopted.

It was very strange. I was 33 and I'd just had one child when Christine, my stepbrother's wife, died. He was drinking very heavily, so I went and picked him up at his house and brought him to my house and we were sitting talking.

He said, "I can't figure why you're the one to come and pick me up."

I said, "Well why wouldn't I? I'm your sister."

"You're my step-sister."

I said, "Yeah, but you were from my mother's first husband."

He said, "No, you were adopted."

Well, I was in a state of shock. I couldn't believe it. Then I remembered that when I was having trouble conceiving a child, my mother said to me, "Why don't you adopt?"

I said, "Well, Jerry being a Greek, I don't think he'd ever go for adopting a child."

She said, "Well, you know your sister, Tanis is adopted."

I said, "Oh, my goodness."

I thought about that. "What are you ever going to tell her if she ever finds out and asks you about it?"

She said, "I'll just tell her that you're adopted."

I said, "You know, Mum, there was a woman that used to come into the office all the time, and she said to me, 'Which one of you girls is the adopted one?' and I kept saying to her that none of us were adopted. She said, 'No, no, no, one of Wes VanDeusen's girls is adopted.'"

But I never questioned it. I thought I had solved it. Tanis was adopted, but she never knew it. She died young and she never knew it.

By the time I found out about me, my mother had died. My father was still alive, but I didn't want to go to him, because I thought that if he had wanted me to know he would have told me. So I went to my older sister, Aleta, who was not adopted. She was their child for sure. I said, "This is what Len's told me."

She said, "This is not true. Absolutely not true."

I said, "Okay, that's fine."

So I phoned my cousin, Fran. I told her what Len said, and she said, "I'll ask my Dad."

That was my father's brother.

She came back, "Nope. Absolutely; you're not adopted."

So I thought, "Okay, there's one person in this wide world who will tell me about this. My mother's sister, Aunt Mary." She was in a seniors' home in California in Orange County. To this day I try to go in my mind and figure out, how did I do this? How did I find the address? How did I find her?

But I got on a plane, got to LA, rented a car, drove to the retirement home and went up to her room. She was there, and she knew who I was.

I said, "Aunt Mary, this is what Len Hardy told me."

"Your mother would kill him for telling you. Yes, you were adopted. Your mother had a stillborn child, a boy. She was all set for this boy, and she decided she was going to have a baby in that house, regardless. You know how your mother loved to shop. Well, we went shopping for a baby. We found you at the General Hospital just up the street from Acme Novelty. She phoned your father and said, 'Wes, I think I've got the one. You'd better come down here.' It was about a block away. So he went up and they adopted you."

So I became a Van Deusen. Wasn't I a lucky girl.

And here's the other funny thing. There were three girls. Tannis was adopted. Her birthday was the third of August. Leave out the fourth. Aleta was born the fifth. Leave out the sixth. I'm the seventh of August.

I'm thinking, "My mother was a businesswoman. She just wanted to keep it simple. We'll just have one birthday party and Bob's your uncle."

So then my children knew that I was adopted, and they made me promise that once my father passed away that I would find out – for health reasons – who my parents were.

When my mother died, my father had remarried, a wonderful woman by the name of Ruth who had two adopted children. So I talked to her.

I said, "I know I'm adopted. I'd like to talk to Dad about it. "

She said, "Don't ever do it. As far as he considers, you are his child, and he does not want to talk about it."

So that was fine.

Then my Dad died. I was in Arizona with my son and his wife, and Adam said, "It's time."

I said, "Okay. Aunt Mary told me I was born at the General Hospital in Edmonton, the Misericordia."

So I wrote to the hospital, "This was when I think I was born, who I was adopted by, and blah, blah, blah."

Anyways, I get these papers back, with all this information. So my mother was a housekeeper in Barhead, Alberta. My father was a truck driver. They never got married.

And I started searching for my mother's family, the Macleans. I phoned Barhead, looking for anyone with the name of Maclean or Munier, which was my father's name. I talked to his brother. He did not remember his brother dating my mother. I couldn't find any of her family.

I then traced them to having lived up around some lake in northern BC. I wrote to a newspaper there. Their name was Maclean, and they owned a hotel in the town. So I wrote to the newspaper editor about trying to find my mother.

She wrote back that she didn't really know anything about them. But on the bottom of her email was a letter from a man by the name of Herd, who was trying to find his mother's child; their name was Maclean. There was his email address.

I emailed him. "Is there any chance that your mother, Eena, is related to May Ellen Maclean?"

He wrote back. "Yes, they're sisters."

So I wrote back. "Is May Ellen alive?"

"Yes, she lives in Kamloops. I will write to her immediately and tell her that you're trying to reach her."

He wrote back immediately. "She's waiting for your phone call. Here's her number."

So I phoned her. So I am now sixty years old, she is eighty. She'd had me when she was twenty. We talked, and it was so wonderful.

I said, "I'm coming to see you."

She was living with my half-sister. So my daughter and her four children and I got in the car and drove to Kamloops and stayed in a hotel and went to visit her. She had been looking for me. Her daughters had encouraged her to look for me. They had gone to see the movie Love Story, and they said, "You're not very moved by this whole thing." And she said, "I have my own love story." And she told them about me.

But she made up a story that her fiancée was killed in the war. But he wasn't, in fact, so she took me aside, "Don't tell them who your father was."

Anyways, her daughters had encouraged her to look for me, and she tried for about two years, but then she said, "You have your own life, you're probably happy, so I just let it go."

So we had a couple of really good visits. Then I got ahold of my half-brother on my father's side, Dwayne. My father had died of bone cancer at about forty-six years old. It turns out I am Metis. I even have a card. But it turns out you don't get any deals.

But my daughter's children filled in a form. They live in Langley, and they go to school there. At the beginning of the year they get a form, "Do you have any native blood?"

Well, because they have native blood, they get a free chocolate bar and pizza every month. And they take them on these lavish field trips. They took them to this beautiful fishing lodge. They took them horseback riding. They took them to Bridges Restaurant in Vancouver.

My mother named me Rosie Marilyn. The Van Deusens kept the name Marilyn. Her name was Mary Ellen, and they named me Marilyn Ellen. I don't know if it was coincidence. But I was born in August, and they didn't "take possession" until December, so I don't know if it took that long to do the paperwork or what, but I was with my mother in Misericordia Hospital. She was working at the hospital and she asked the nuns, "Please don't put her in the nursery," but they did. She said she'd put all the other babies to sleep, then she'd take me in her arms and sit in the rocking chair.

It must have been very, very hard on her. But the interesting thing was that, once I found everything out, it was a joke in the family, because my mother, Helen Van Deusen, was a little bit tippy nose, and she had told anyone who knew that I was adopted that my parents were university students who got in trouble, because that sounded really good.

So anyways, I phoned my uncle Bryce, and I said, "So, here's the good news. I have Metis blood. My mother was a housekeeper and my dad was a truck driver."

And he killed himself laughing. "They were supposed to be university students."

"Well, they weren't."

10. John Palin – A Close Shave

One bombing trip was to Magdeburg, and there were a lot of night fighters out that night. When we got over the target there was a night fighter around, and the mid-upper gunner and myself we had our guns trained on him when another fighter came in from another angle and he fired a cannon shell and tracers, and this cannon shell exploded just below the tail of the plane.

The concussion from it blew all the plastic out of my turret, and my turret doors off, and also affected my eardrums, which I'm now paying for. Also it started a fire that burnt my parachute, which was hanging in the back of the plane. My gun wouldn't work because on the Halifax bombers the guns operated electronically, and the electrics were cut. We were in a bad mess.

We flew back. Fortunately we didn't have any more attacks. We got out over the English Chanel, and the flight engineer said we were getting very low on gas. So the pilot sent out a Mayday distress call and he was directed to the nearest Air Force station in England, which just happened to be a fighter drome. Unfortunately Fighter dromes have shorter runways. He eventually got the plane down after three attempts, but we just kept coasting along. Fortunately also there was nothing at the end of the runway, so we just crashed through the fence and went across farmers' field until we came to a little ditch which brought us to a stop with my tail up in the air. All the crews came out from the fighter station. They got me out of the tail all right. I was too high up to get out myself.

The other crewmembers went out the door over the wing and they got out okay. But anyway were home and landed safely. They gave us accommodation overnight and sent a message through to our squadron that we were all okay.

There's a turret door, which was about 18 inches high, which you could get through with great difficulty. I got in on the right-hand side of the plane. It was a little ladder we climbed up into the plane. That's how all the crew got in. Then they went to their positions at the front, and the mid-upper gunner went to his place, and I had to climb over the tail spar and open my door and then there was a handle there, which you could grab and swing yourself in. I hung my parachute on the side of the plane, because there wasn't room to climb in with it on. All the crew wore their parachute harnesses, but they kept their parachutes close by wherever they were stationed.

When the plane was hit, I couldn't get back into the rest of the plane, so I was stuck out there in the cold at about 250 miles an hour. It was so cold that the metal on my oxygen mask froze to the side of my face.

Fortunately the oxygen was still working, because without that we would have had to go down and fly around five to ten thousand feet, which is more dangerous and uses more fuel.

But we got back okay, but our plane was beyond repair without sending it back to the factory.

So they got us another plane and we did another two trips to Berlin to make up five operations within January and February, '44. I have some data that was released from Bomber Command that says how many bombers went on a raid, and the losses, and there was about 245, 4-engine bombers lost during the time we did those five trips.

11. Jamie Long – Harder Than it Looks

I guess I always was a climber. I know my Mother used to say, quite often, "Don't watch him and he won't get hurt." We'd be out at someone's house, and I'd be out there up the closest tree.

This progressed with scrambling or rock climbing as you'd call it. I spend a lot of summers out at Molice Lake Camp where there was a knoll that was called Stick Hill. I was seven or eight, and I had gone out with my mother early – she was the swimming instructor and played all the music for the singalongs at night on her accordion.

So I went out with the Senior Boys' Camp. The Senior Boys climbed Stick Hill, which was a couple of hundred feet of rock scramble. There were two ways up: you could go up the face or by trail around the back. Of course the Seniors went up the rock face. My brothers Sandy and Gordon scrambled up the face, and me, being the little brother, just went along. This was nothing to me. I didn't seem to have any fear of 150 feet down or anything like that. We weren't using ropes or anything.

That was all well and good until I hit Junior Camp and I was with my peers. We hit Stick Hill and the little kids were supposed to take the trail around the back side, which was much safer than going up the face.

Of course, as soon as we got out of the vehicles at the bottom, I took a contingent of my buddies and we went running up the face. The counsellors were freaking out, calling us, "Come back, come back!"

We pretended not to hear them, and scrambled to the top. Of course, I was in deep crap when we got back down the mountain.

So anyway, the years pass, and I'm always happy to climb whatever mountain that comes to pass.

I ended up going up to the Yukon as a finishing log builder. My Dad had been teaching a log-building course, and a gentleman named Hector Mackenzie was working with me. He professed to be a climber, and in fact this father was an internationally known climber in Europe. On the weekends, when Hector wasn't on the course with my father, he was out climbing in the mountains around White Horse.

I bugged him. I wanted to go climbing with him.

"Oh, I'm pretty technical," he said. "I don't think you'd want to go with me, because I do some pretty steep pitches, and for a novice it would be…"

"Oh, I'm not a novice. I've climbed lots," I say, from my big ego and whatever else.

Hector says, "Well, okay, then, Buddy, we'll see how you make out."

So we went out, only about 30 miles from White Horse, and there were these three pitches of about 100 feet each that we were going to climb up.

I looked at them, and I'm going, "Holy crap. I mean what have I got myself into?"

And I'll tell you, what I got myself into was nothing but trouble. The only boots that I had were steel-toed boots. This is a steel cap on the end of your boot, and when you're in a rock face position and your foot's in there holding on with your toe, that steel cap is crimping off your circulation on the top of your foot.

So we'd done two pitches, and I could feel myself getting exhausted. We had one more to go, about a hundred feet, and it's a little past 90 degrees. We were all roped off, and I had total confidence in Hector's ability to save my ass if I fell. That's the one good thing I had going for me; that was it, really.

But as I'm climbing I'm feeling my stamina draining out the bottoms of my boots because of the pain from being pinched off on the top of my foot by the steel toe.

We'd made it virtually to the top, and we were going up a small chimney, and then there was the top, and Hector was up on the top of the pitch and I'm in a plaintive voice saying, "Hector, I can't find a handhold. There's no handhold!"

Hector looks down in this Scottish brogue and says, "There's always a handhold, young fella."

"No there's not!" and I'm feeling exhausted. And all of a sudden I had nothing left in me. I had nothing in my feet. I only had a very, very short pitch to go. I don't think I had more than about two feet before I was at the very, very top, but no handhold.

I said, "That's it. I'm goin' for it." And unbeknownst to Hector – he didn't know what I was going to do – I just jumped. He had to scramble to pull me up.

And then he stripped me out like you'd never believe. "You don't do that. You never do that. Whatever else, you never do that."

And I'm just sitting there at the top of the pitch saying, "I made it. I made it."

So to tell the truth, that kinda did me for mountaineering. That was the thing, and I've never pursued it. I've never gone into ropes or that sort of thing. That was the first time I've ever used ropes, and it was my last.

12. John Palin – Heroism

In August 1944 Bomber Command was told through intelligence that there was a large supply depot of the flying bombs that were really causing a lot of problems in England, so they ordered Bomber Command to go out and drop flares, but they couldn't find it, so they had to come home with their bombs. They went out again another night a couple of days later, and still couldn't find the place. This was all happening in one week. Around Thursday or Friday of that week they ordered 60 bombers from Pathfinder squadrons to go out and destroy that place in daylight. So we went out and it was destroyed and there was quite a bit of flak from anti-aircraft fire round the place. They weren't expecting a daylight raid, but they still threw up quite a defense.

Anyway, one of the planes from our squadron got hit by flak, and the fire started and the fire got out of control. The pilot ordered the crew to bail out but two of the crewmembers were wounded by the flak and they couldn't get out of the plane. So the other four bailed out and the pilot and the two wounded ones were left. He was going to try to land his plane on a little field just a few miles from the target area. He landed all right, but as soon as he landed the plane blew up, and he had bombs aboard and fuel, and the plane blew up and they were all killed. Once the crew members who bailed out were released from the prisoner of war camp later, they reported the story of what he tried to do, and he was awarded the Victoria Cross. There was a nice writeup about it. I have a copy of it.

After D-Day and the end of the war in 1945 we all came back. I came back on the Ile de France, a nice big ocean liner. Far more comfortable than when I went over.

13. Morgan Gadd – Something Happened on Cottontail

The year is 1967, I'm 18 going on 19 years old, and we're climbing in the desert. The group of six of us are climbing in the desert of Utah. We've climbed these red sandstone formations before. These are red...I guess you could say they're skyscrapers standing in the middle of the desert. They're red, sandstone towers. In Utah, near Moab, there's a cluster of them, about 6 towers. Other climbers were climbing in them. There had been some first ascents. One of them was called The Titan, another was called The Echo. Another tower was called Cottontail. This tower – it was about a thousand feet tall – had a big boulder on the middle of top that looked like the tail of a rabbit.

Our objective was to do a first ascent of this tower. Over a period of about 6 days, we did that. But it wasn't without incident, and I want to say a few words about a very significant incident that happened with me, as a member of this climbing team.

Climbing this tower is probably the most difficult climbing you can do. What we call F-12 or A-1 or A-6. It's freestyle climbing mixed with direct aid climbing. It's very complex technical climbing at the highest quality. That's the kind of stuff we were doing. We would actually sleep in our little hanging stretchers on the rock face.

We'd take turns leading the climb, and it came to my turn to lead. We were up near the top already. We'd been climbing for a number of days, probably about 800 feet, and it was my turn to take the lead. I came out around a kind of a corner, and I saw a crack system going up above me, and I began to climb up this crack system.

What is interesting about this sandstone is that it's very old rock, and over the millenia it has been standing there and eroding, so the surface of the rock is coated with a kind of a mud layer. You wouldn't see it until you got right up close to it, but it's basically rotten rock, like a skin of rotten mud sandstone on top of the good sandstone. So in order to climb it, we would have to very carefully clear that mud layer off, and when we put in our protection we had to clear these layers off, put in the protection and then climb.

So as we're climbing the route we're actually cleaning the rock to make it easy for the people following us. So there's stuff always falling down from the leader, who is always kicking stuff and breaking this crust that was on the surface of the rock

This rock had an interesting feature; it would go in kind of bumps or bands. As you were climbing up you would come to a band of harder rock that stuck out, and you were climbing up over a rounded overhang that you would have to follow and go over. Normally you would put in direct aid there. We would drill holes, put in bolts, and use that to go over the overhang to get on top of it, and keep on going up vertically.

I came up to a fairly large overhang, and I got ready to put in my direct aid. By now I was probably 15 to 20 feet past where I started my climb, and I'd put in some protection, some pitons, but I knew that those pitons were not very good. I was pretty sure that if I did fall, I would probably take a really long fall, probably 50 feet, and then slam into the rock below. That could be a killer fall. It would knock you out, and could kill you. It could pull everybody off the rock, actually. Very dangerous. I knew it was not safe. I didn't like the feeling of it, but I just had to trust that I had done my piton protection properly.

So I came up to the overhang, and I jammed one hand into the crack that went right through this overhang for stability, and I got ready to knock the piton in so I could put in the protection. As I was doing that, I've got both hands over my head.

I've got one hand in the crack, the other hand has the hammer with the piton, I'm putting it in...and my feet began to break out on this muddy crust.

And I knew that in my mind I said, "This is it. I'm gone." Everything in my mind prepared me for a major-disaster-type fall. Probably death. I wouldn't be surprised if I were dead from this.

And then everything just blanked out. I mean, it just blanked out. All I know is that I came to my senses and I was huddled in a kind of wind-blown pocket in the sandstone, like a window. You know how the wind will erode potholes in the sandstone. I was cuddled, curled up inside one of these little stone windows. I was shaking like a leaf. The rope trailed off below me and disappeared. I didn't know how I got there.

I had actually gone over the overhang and travelled another 10 or 15 feet up to this pocket, and basically got to safety. And I had no idea how I got there. I just came to, and there I was. Tucked in there.

So when I realized, I gave thanks I was still alive. I didn't know how that happened, but it did, and because there were no cracks, now; the crack system was gone. I put in a bolt to tie myself off, to anchor myself, getting ready to bring up the rope. The team of climbers would come up to me next, and that was the end of that lead of climbing.

As I was preparing this I was thinking, "What happened? What happened?" But all I can describe is that it felt like I just merged, that my consciousness just merged with the overall feeling of oneness, of complete unity, completely being a part. I didn't separate myself from the rock kind of feeling. I was a part of every little thing. And every little thing was a part of me. It was this amazing moment of awareness where everything just blended into one.

And then I came out of it into this awareness that I'm an individual tucked into this pocket in the stone.

So that's the only way I can describe that feeling, and thankfulness that I was alive. People say that's a very unusual experience. People get these in extreme situations like car accidents and plane crashes, and things happen and "All I know is I felt like I became one with everything during this moment."

So when I had finished putting in the bolt I called down, "Off climb!" and I began to belay the next person on the team who was coming up below me. Now I'm taking up the rope as this person is coming. And he got to where the overhang was, and he said, "Morgan, what did you do here? How did you climb this? Did you climb this free?"

I said, "I don't know how, but I did."

I had to pull him up over about a three-foot overhang,

He was amazed and so was everyone else who came up. They said, "That's impossible, what you did." Because there were no handholds: nothing, there. They said, "Whatever you did, there, it's unexplainable. It's impossible. It defies gravity. You just can't do that."

At that moment, something happened. You could call this story, "Something Happened."

I don't know what it was, except I'm alive to tell the tale. I don't know how or why, but it's one of those great mysterious moments in my life that I can never forget. I can recall that moment very easily. It was one of those life-changing kind of moments.

This was the Climb on Cottontail, Moab, Utah.

Book 4 Participants:

1. Eve Baldwin

Eve was born in 1925 in England. She spent her childhood years in India, joined the British Air Force during WWII, and has led an adventurous life ever since. (23, 26, 29, 31, 33, 34, 45, 80, 81)

2. Roger Barnes

My name is Roger Barnes. I was born in Widnes, England in 1946. Close to the Liverpool/Manchester area. (5)

3. David Barregar

My name is David Barregar I was born in Rouleau, in the French part of Saskatchewan, on 29 December, 1933. I served in Intelligence with the Canadian Air Force and was a well-known broadcaster with CBC Radio in Calgary. My lifetime hobby has been flying. (14, 79)

4. Tom Brown

I was born in 1923 up in Willoughby, and I lived there until I was three years old, when we moved down to on 200th at the foot of the hill. In total we had 8 children in our family, four girls and four boys. I grew up when Dad was logging with horses, and I loved being out in the woods with the horses. I spent my life logging, building logging roads, and working on logging equipment. I was married for 69 years and raised 2 children. (41)

5. Joan Campbell

I was born in 1919 in a tiny village called Chinnor in the Chiltern Hills in the south of England. My grandfather was a minister of the Church of England. My father died leading his men out of the trenches in WW I, so I grew up in my grandfather's rectory. (1, 38, 42)

6. Eva

Eva is from Mexico. She and her husband, Benjamin, sent their three children, one by one, to Canada to learn English. Now the whole family lives here. (1)

7. Morgan Gadd

Morgan is a retired educator with a long career in academic and professional theatre. He believes that expressing oneself through the arts can be a life-affirming and a life-saving activity. (93)

8. Marilyn Gerald

My name is Marilyn Gerald. I was born in Edmonton Alberta, August 7, 1940 to Helen and Wes VanDeusen. I went to school at Garneau Elementary School in Edmonton. My father and mother were the founders of Acme Novelty Company in Edmonton. (9, 11, 78, 85)

9. Mavis Holt

My full name is Mavis Bertha Caroline Holt. I was born in Wainwright Alberta, in 1937. I now live in Langley Lodge, where I do a lot of volunteering. (12)

10. The Johnston Family: Dave, Janice, Hal

Dave and Janice Johnston are both from Vancouver, born and raised. They met in High School, married, and had three children, Hal, Judi, and Charles. They are a long-time Vancouver boating family. (65-74)

11. Bernadette Law

I was born in Hong Kong. I came to Canada to study Art at university, and have lived in Alberta and British Columbia ever since. I am a member of the Surrey Seniors' Planning Table. (17)

12. Gordon Long

Gordon has retired from teaching in Prince George to live in Tsawwassen, be a member of the Surrey Seniors' Planning Table and...edit this book. (76)

13. Jamie Long

Jamie is a carpenter living in Nanaimo and working in the Oil Patch in Alberta. (6, 90)

14. Karen MacGregor

Karen is Norm Schmidt's daughter. She is a hairdresser in Surrey, and active in Whaley Little League. (27, 35, 38, 80)

15. Josie McGinnis

My name is Josie McGinnis. I live in Delta, B. C. I'm a widow, retired on the pension I fought for after my husband died a few days before his 55th birthday. (83)

16. John Palen

John is a decorated WWII veteran and retired nursing home administrator. He was born Dec 1, 1922, in the Village of Haliburton Ontario. (13, 49, 51, 53, 89, 92)

17. Leo Ramirez

Originally I'm from El Salvadore. I came to Canada on October 5 of 1984. I landed in Toronto with my family:hree kids – two boys, one girl – and my wife. Before coming to Canada I was a journalist. (84)

18. Norm Schmidt

Norm Schmidt opened the first Optometry clinic in Surrey in the 1950s. He married in 1955 and had four children. (16, 54-64)

19. Cal Whitehead

Cal was born in Canada, in Vancouver, in 1926. After making several careers in Ontario, he returned to B. C. in 2001 to spend time with his mother. He died in May 2017, after contributing many stories, long and short, serious and not so serious, to the ElderStory Project. He will be sorely missed by all of us. (15, 16,)

20. Faye Whitehead

My name is Fay. My maiden name was duBois. My father came from Northern Ireland, so we're Huguenot descendants. Dad came to Canada when he was 16. I never did ask him why. He was the oldest boy in the family and why would he leave them? I'm curious about that now, and it's too late. (21, 24)

ElderStory Committee

Gordon A. Long

Gordon is the recording technician, storytelling coach and editor of the ElderStory Project. He was born and raised in Palling, a small farming community near Burns Lake, B. C. He is a retired teacher, a playwright, director and acting teacher, and the self-published author of 9 novels. He has been a member of the Planning Table since 2011.

Judith McBride

Judith is the administrator of the Planning Table and the ElderStory Project. She was born in South London, England in the winter of 1949. She moved to Canada in 1974, settling in B.C in 1976. She has worked for the last 40 years in charitable & nonprofit endeavours.

Fiona Stevenson

Fiona is the Manager of Volunteer and Community Programs at DIVERSEcity Community Resources Society. She oversees a diverse portfolio of programs from settlement and integration to food security and seniors' initiatives. She has been a member and supporter of the Surrey Seniors' Planning Table since 2017.

The ElderStory Project

This project was conceived by the Planning Table, supported by DIVERSEcity, and funded by the New Horizons for Seniors program of the Government of Canada.

First we held recording sessions, for individuals and groups of storytellers in KinVillage in Tsawwassen, DIVERSEcity offices in Surrey, in Langley Lodge and in people's homes.

A second part involved our storytelling coach giving workshops in Woodward Hill and Surrey Centre elementary schools. At an evening storytelling session students, teachers and parents were then invited to tell their family stories.

Now the stories have been transcribed and will be made into a series of books.

Surrey Seniors' Planning Table

The Surrey Seniors' Planning table is an organization of seniors dedicated to connecting seniors with the community. We accomplish projects involving multicultural and multigenerational cooperation and try to enhance the lives of Seniors and promote an age-friendly community.

Other Planning Table members in the ElderStory Project:

Beverly-Jean Brunet	Bernadette Law
Luz Lopezdee	Kay Noonan
Mohammed Rafiq	Roslyn Simon
Evelyn Wallenborn	

DIVERSEcity

DIVERSEcity Community Resources Society, established in 1978, is a not-for-profit agency offering a wide range of services and programs to the culturally diverse communities of the lower mainland. DIVERSEcity prides itself on its well-founded expertise in assisting immigrants and new Canadians in their integration into their new community. Our programs continue to expand and change to reflect the unique needs of the diverse community we serve. We have a strong commitment to raising awareness of the economic and cultural contributions immigrants make to Canadian society, and to raising awareness of the value of diversity.

New Horizons for Seniors

The New Horizons for Seniors Program is a federal Grants and Contributions program that supports projects led or inspired by seniors who make a difference in the lives of others and in their communities. By supporting a variety of opportunities for seniors, the New Horizons for Seniors Program works to better the lives of all Canadians. Since its creation in 2004, the Program has helped seniors lead and participate in activities across the country.

Made in the USA
Columbia, SC
27 January 2019